Football's Most Wanted

Also by Floyd Conner

Baseball's Most Wanted: The Top 10 of the National Pastime's Outrageous Offenders, Lucky Bounces, and Other Oddities

Golf!

Fore!

This Date in Sports History

Day by Day in Cincinnati Reds History

Day by Day in Cincinnati Bengals History

Pretty Poison

Lupe Velez and Her Lovers

Football's Most Wanted

The Top 10 Book of the Game's Outrageous Characters, Fortunate Fumbles, and Other Oddities

Floyd Conner

Brassey's

WASHINGTON, D.C.

Library of Congress Cataloging-in-Publication Data

Conner, Floyd, 1951–
Football's most wanted : the top 10 book of the great game's outrageous characters, fortunate fumbles, and other oddities / Floyd Conner.– 1st ed.
p. cm.
Includes bibliographical references.
ISBN 1-57488-309-7 (alk. paper)
1. Football–Miscellanea. 2. Football players–Anecdotes. I. Title: Top 10 book of the great game's outrageous characters, fortunate fumbles, and other oddities. II. Title.

GV950.5 .C65 2000
796.332–dc21 00-062151

Printed in Canada on acid-free paper that meets the American National Standards Institute Z39-48 Standard

Brassey's
22841 Quicksilver Drive
Dulles, Virginia 20166

Designed by Pen & Palette Unlimited

First Edition

10 9 8 7 6 5 4 3 2 1

Contents

List of Photographs xi

Introduction 1

First Downs 5
Famous football firsts

Screen Passes 10
From screen passes to the silver screen

Made for TV 15
They were ready for prime time

Playing Politics 20
They threw their helmets into the ring

Covering All Bases 25
Stars of the gridiron and diamond

Basket Cases 29
Football players with hoop dreams

Going for the Gold 34
Olympic medalists who played football

Gridiron Grapplers 37
Wrestling is as easy as one, two, three

Intellectual Assassins 41
Football's smart set

Paper Lions 45
Football pros and literary prose

Slippery Rock and Walla Walla 49
Small-college alumni

What Might Have Been 53
Great careers cut short

Heisman Busts 57
Players who didn't live up to expectations

Draft Steals 60
High draft choices who made it big

The Undrafted 65
Their names weren't called on draft day

Football's Jackie Robinsons 69
African-American football pioneers

Outrageous Owners 73
The noteworthy and notorious

Crazy Legs and Tippy Toes 78
The game's most memorable nicknames

The Name Game 82
These men were born to play football

Mad Storks 85
Football's fabulous flakes

Practical Jokers 90
All-pro pranksters

Memorable Mascots 94
Dogs, goats, and an irate ibis

Uniform Behavior 98
Clothes made these men

Good Things Come in Small Packages 102
Football's mighty mites

Heavyweights 105
Bigger than a refrigerator

Meal Tickets 108
They were what they ate

Drinking It All In 112
Players who drank more than Gatorade

Making Passes 116
They had all the moves

One-Game Wonders 120
The game of their lives

The Best Year of their Lives 124
Their one year in the sun

The One and Only 127
One-of-a-kind achievements

Sixty-Minute Men 130
They played both ways

You Can Look It Up: College 134
Little-known collegiate records

You Can Look It Up: Pro 138
Pro football's unheralded records

Records Which May Never Be Broken 141
These records weren't meant to be broken

The Worst Plays of All Time 145
Bad calls, costly fumbles, and wrong-way runs

The Offense Rests 149
The least offensive performances in football history

Losing's the Only Thing 152
For every winning coach, there's a loser

Unorthodox Coaches 155
Gloomy Gil and Weeping Wally

Seasons to Forget 160
The worst teams of all time

Running up the Score 164
Football's biggest blowouts

Unusual Bowl Games 168
Iodine, Kickapoo, and Chigger Bowls

Steamrollers and Eskimos 171
The NFL's most unlikely franchises

Believe It or Nots 175
Anything can happen at a football game

Strange Plays 179
Just when you think you've seen it all

The Strangest Games Ever Played 183
Football's most unbelievable games

Not Fit for Man nor Beast 187
Ice, snow, and fog bowls

Whistle Blowers 191
Arguments for instant replay

Football's Most Embarrassing Moments 195
They could run but could not hide

Ultimate Upsets 199
These teams overcame the odds

Not So Super Performances 203
Super Bowl performances they'd rather forget

They Never Won the Super Bowl 207
Superstars who never won the big one

Unlikely Super Heroes 210
They rose to the occasion

Instant Replays 213
Unforgettable football broadcasts

Overcoming Handicaps 216
Physical handicaps couldn't stop them

Incredible Injuries 219
Adding insult to injury

Serious Injuries 223
Football can be a dangerous game

Tough Guys 227
The sport's indestructible men

Hard Hitters 230
Football is a collision sport

Personal Fouls 234
They sometimes played dirty

Bending the Rules 238
Rules are meant to be broken

It's a Gamble 242
You can bet on it

Illegal Substances 246
Victims of substance abuse

Crime and Football 249
They crossed the line

Fanatics 253
Football's most rabid fans

Death in the Afternoon 257
Football fatalities

Dead Before Their Times 260
Gone too soon

Out with a Bang 264
They saved their best for last

Fantastic Finishes 267
Last-second heroics

Bibliography 271

Index 275

List of Photographs

John Wayne	11
Bill Cosby	16
Charlie Ward	30
David Klingler	135
Dan Marino	143
Jerry Glanville	177
Sterling Sharpe	225
Randy Moss	251
Derrick Thomas	262

Introduction

Football has become the most popular sport in America. The National Football League has come a long way from its humble origins 80 years ago. In 1920, a pro football franchise could be purchased for a mere $100. One of the charter teams, the Racine Cardinals, was named for a street in Chicago. The Oorang Indians' main purpose was to publicize a dog kennel in LaRue, Ohio. The Racine (Wisconsin) Legion were sponsored by an American Legion post. Today, a franchise such as the Washington Redskins is valued at $800 million.

Football's Most Wanted recognizes the sport's most outrageous characters. The book contains top-ten lists of the worst players, losingest coaches, and craziest plays in college and professional football history. The lists feature the unlikeliest heroes, most outlandish stunts, wildest fans, toughest players, fantastic finishes, and the strangest things ever to occur on a football field.

It is a game in which the most unsung player can become a star. Undrafted Kurt Warner, given an opportunity because of an injury to the starting quarterback, became the 1999 National Football League Most Valuable Player and led the St. Louis Rams to victory in Super Bowl XXXIV. Johnny Unitas, a ninth-round draft pick cut by the Pittsburgh Steelers, later became a superstar quarterback with the Baltimore Colts. George Blanda, a 12th-round draft pick in 1949, played a record 26 seasons as a professional.

Almost anything can happen in a football game. In 1893, T.L. Bayne coached both Louisiana State and Tulane in a game he also refereed. Oklahoma's Ed Cook literally swam for a touchdown in a 1904 game against Oklahoma A&M. The University of the South defeated five major college teams in a span of six days in 1899. The Rose Bowl football game was replaced by such events as chariot racing and tent pegging from 1903 to 1905. Some unusual bowl games of the past include the Spaghetti Bowl, Turkey Bowl, Iodine Bowl, Fish Bowl, Kickapoo Bowl, Refrigerator Bowl, Arab Bowl, and the Chigger Bowl.

Several college and professional players have gone on to successful political careers. President Dwight Eisenhower was a starting halfback for Army before a knee injury derailed his career. Another future president, Gerald Ford, was a star center at the University of Michigan. Massachusetts Senator Ted Kennedy caught two touchdown passes for Harvard during his college career. Jack Kemp, the 1996 Republican vice presidential candidate, quarterbacked the Buffalo Bills to an American Football League championship. Former football stars J.C. Watts and Steve Largent are rising stars in American politics.

Football can be a dangerous game. In 1940, Washington Redskins' Hall of Fame tackle Turk Edwards suffered a career-ending knee injury during a coin toss. Clive Rush was electrocuted in 1969 when he grabbed a live microphone after being introduced as the Boston Patriots' new head coach. In

1931, Texas Christian coach Francis Schmidt did a back flip when he forgot to take off his headphones and ran onto the field to argue a call. Even the team mascot isn't safe. Bevo, the first Texas Longhorns' steer mascot, was eaten at the team's postseason banquet in 1920.

This book introduces you to nearly 700 of football's most wanted players. Their offenses range from inept play to outrageous behavior. Be on the lookout for these individuals.

FIRST DOWNS

The first games in the history of the National Football League (then called the American Professional Football Association) were played on October 3, 1920. On that day, the Rock Island Independents shut out the Muncie Flyers 45–0, and the Dayton Triangles defeated the Columbus Panhandles 14–0. The following is a list of notable football firsts.

1. WALTER CAMP

Walter Camp has been called the "Father of American Football." Before Walter Camp, American football was just a version of the English game rugby. Camp introduced a number of innovations that revolutionized the game. He reduced the number of players on a side from 15 to 11 and devised the down system which controls the possession of the ball. In 1889, he created the first College All-American Team. As a coach, he was unrivaled. During his first five seasons as a head coach, from 1888 to 1892, his teams at Yale and Stanford had a record of 69 wins, 2 losses, and 2 ties. His three undefeated teams outscored their opponents 1,621–0.

2. PUDGE HEFFELFINGER

The first professional football player was William "Pudge" Heffelfinger. An All-American at Yale from 1889 to 1891, Heffelfinger is credited with being the first pulling guard. He was such a great lineman that the Allegheny Athletic Association team of Pittsburgh agreed to pay him $500 to play for them in a game against the Pittsburgh Athletic Club on November 12, 1892. It marked the first time in football history that a player had been paid to participate in a game. To put the amount of the payment in perspective, the team spent only $50 to rent the field on which the game was played. The investment proved to be a wise one as Heffelfinger forced a fumble and returned it 35 yards for the game's only touchdown (which then was worth four points) as Allegheny defeated Pittsburgh by the score of 4–0. In 1916, at the age of 48, Pudge was still tough enough to knock out five players during a scrimmage with Yale players. Four years later, he played 56 minutes in an all-star charity game against college players. One player was so impressed by Heffelfinger's fitness and endurance that he asked to see his birth certificate.

3. JAY BERWANGER

Jay Berwanger, an All-American running back for the University of Chicago, was the first recipient of the Heisman Trophy in 1935. Runners-up in the balloting were Monk Meyer of Army, Notre Dame halfback Bill Shakespeare, and Princeton fullback Pepper Constable. For the first year only players from colleges east of the Mississippi were considered for the Heisman Trophy. Subsequently, the award was presented to the best college player in the country. On February 8, 1936, Berwanger was the first player picked in the inaugural National Football League draft. Selected by the Philadelphia

Eagles, the rights to Berwanger were traded to the Chicago Bears. The Bears refused to sign him after he demanded a two-year contract for the then-unheard-of sum of $20,000. At the time, draft picks signed for as little as $125. Berwanger never played professional football but made a fortune in the rubber business.

4. **PAUL BROWN**

Paul Brown was professional football's greatest innovator. As a high school coach at Massillon High School in Ohio, Brown's team was so good that once they went the entire season without having to punt. During the four years of the All-America Football Conference, from 1946 to 1949, Brown coached Cleveland to league championships every year. In 1950, the Cleveland Browns joined the National Football League. During his first six years in the NFL, Brown's teams won three championships and were in the title game every year. Much of Brown's success can be attributed to numerous innovations, which included full-time coaching staffs, a college scouting network, intelligence tests for players, grading player performances after viewing game films, sending in plays via messengers, and installing a radio transmitter in the helmet of his quarterback. Brown was also one of the first coaches to sign African-American players. Brown later founded a second franchise, the Cincinnati Bengals, in 1968.

5. **RUTGERS**

The first intercollegiate football game was played between Rutgers and Princeton at New Brunswick, New Jersey, on November 6, 1869. With 25 players to a side and goals counting one point each, the rules were quite different from today's game. Rutgers won 6–4.

6. SYRACUSE

The first indoor football game was played in New York's Madison Square Garden on December 28, 1902. The Syracuse Athletic Club defeated New York by the score of 5–0.

7. PROVIDENCE

Professional football's first night game was played between the Providence Steam Roller and the Chicago Cardinals on November 3, 1929. The historic game, played at Providence's Kinsley Park, was won by Chicago 16–0. Football's first game under lights preceded Major League Baseball's first night game, played in Cincinnati, by six years.

8. PETE GOGOLAK

The first soccer-style kicker to play in the National Football League was Pete Gogolak. The native of Budapest, Hungary, played for the Buffalo Bills and New York Giants between 1964 and 1974. Gogolak led the NFL in field goals with 28 in 1965 and for his career accounted for 173 field goals and 344 extra points. Soccer-style kickers were able to kick the ball farther and with more accuracy than straight-on kickers.

Soccer-style kickers differ from the conventional place kicker by advancing on the ball from an angle and kicking the ball with the side of their foot. Today, all professional place-kickers use this soccer style.

9. WALLY TRIPLETT

Wally Triplett was the first African-American draft pick to play in the National Football League. The Penn State halfback was selected in the nineteenth round of the 1949 draft by the Detroit Lions. Triplett played four seasons in the NFL with Detroit and the Chicago Cardinals, rushing for 321 yards and scoring four touchdowns.

10. ERIC SWANN

In 1991, defensive lineman Eric Swann became the first player drafted in the first round without collegiate experience. Swann was drafted by the Phoenix Cardinals after starring for the Bay City Titans, a minor-league football team. He was selected to the NFL Pro Bowl in both 1996 and 1997.

SCREEN PASSES

Football players have been matinee idols since the 1920s. Slingin' Sammy Baugh, the Hall of Fame quarterback, starred in a Republic western, *King of the Texas Rangers,* in 1941. Woody Strode, one of the first African-Americans to play in the National Football League, later starred in two films directed by John Ford, *Sergeant Rutledge* and *The Man who Shot Liberty Valance.* Frank Gifford, star halfback for the New York Giants in the '60s, appeared in numerous films, including *Darby's Rangers* and *Two-Minute Warning.* Kris Kristofferson was a star football player at Pomona College from 1954 to 1957 before becoming an actor and appearing in films such as *A Star Is Born* and *Semi-Tough.* Recently, MVP quarterback Brett Favre of the Green Bay Packers was cast as Cameron Diaz's love interest in the hit comedy *There's Something About Mary.* Other NFL players to appear on the big screen include Dick Butkus, Bubba Smith, Tim Rossovich, Rosey Grier, Joe Klecko, John Matuszak, Lyle Alzado, Howie Long, Kenny Washington, and Brian Bosworth. This list features men who made the transition from the gridiron to the silver screen.

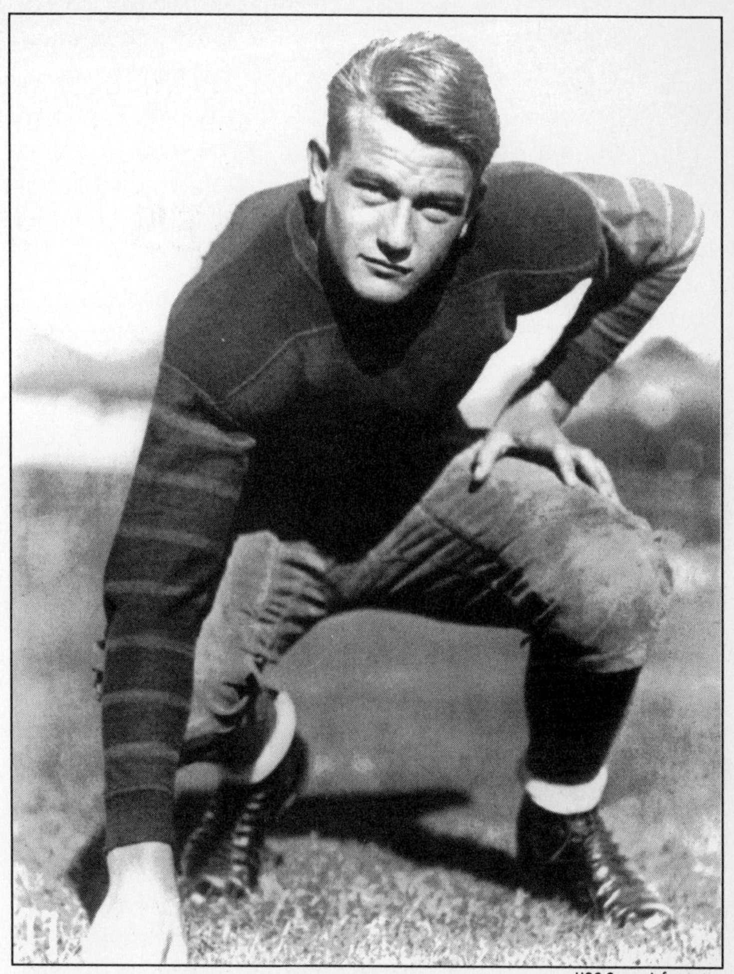

USC Sports Information

John Wayne

Marion Morrison played tackle for the University of Southern California Trojans in 1925 and 1926. Later, as a budding film actor, Twentieth Century Fox persuaded him to change his name to John Wayne, now one of the most legendary names in Hollywood history.

1. JOHN WAYNE

Marion Morrison played tackle for the University of Southern California Trojans in 1925 and 1926. Cowboy star Tom Mix got him a job in the prop department at Fox, and for a time he worked as a set decorator. Tall and brawny, Morrison attracted the attention of directors John Ford and Raoul Walsh. The studio changed his name to John Wayne, and for 50 years he reigned as one of Hollywood's most popular stars. Wayne's most memorable performances occurred in westerns such as *Stagecoach* (1939), *The Searchers* (1956), and *True Grit* (1969), for which he won an Oscar.

2. BURT REYNOLDS

Buddy Reynolds averaged 8.4 yards per carry as running back for the 1954 Florida State freshman team. Reynolds saw limited action on the varsity squad from 1955 to 1957. In Hollywood, Burt Reynolds climbed the ranks from stunt man to television star to the movies' top box-office draw. Reynolds' career has been highlighted by critically acclaimed performances in *Deliverance* and *Boogie Nights.*

3. JIM BROWN

Jim Brown shocked many when he walked away from professional football in 1965 at the age of 29 to pursue an acting career in films. Often considered the greatest player in pro football history, Brown led the league in rushing eight of the nine seasons he played in the NFL. While his Hollywood success never approached his legendary gridiron performance, he did become the first black action star. Brown's screen credits include *The Dirty Dozen, Ice Station Zebra,* and *Mars Attacks.*

4. JOHNNY MACK BROWN

An All-American at Alabama from 1924 to 1926, Johnny Mack Brown caught two touchdown passes for the Crimson Tide in their 1926 Rose Bowl victory over Washington. During his 40-year movie career, Brown appeared in more than 300 films. Brown co-starred with many of Hollywood's most popular leading women, including Greta Garbo, Joan Crawford, and Mary Pickford. He is best remembered for his roles in westerns such as *Billy the Kid, Wells Fargo,* and *Ride 'Em Cowboy.*

5. O.J. SIMPSON

O.J. Simpson was an outstanding running back at the University of Southern California and won the Heisman Trophy in 1968. A four-time NFL rushing champion for the Buffalo Bills, the "Juice" became the first pro player to rush for more than 2,000 yards in 1973. Simpson parlayed his good looks into a successful acting career. He has appeared in numerous films, including *The Towering Inferno, Killer Force,* and *The Naked Gun.*

6. CARL WEATHERS

Carl Weathers played linebacker for the Oakland Raiders in 1970 and 1971. Best known for his portrayal of boxing champion Apollo Creed in *Rocky,* Weathers' film credits include *Predator, Action Jackson,* and *Close Encounters of the Third Kind.*

7. BERNIE CASEY

An outstanding wide receiver for the San Francisco Forty-Niners and Los Angeles Rams from 1961 to 1968, Bernie Casey caught 359 passes and scored 40 touchdowns in his NFL career. Equally successful as an actor, Casey has appeared in many films, notably *Never Say Never Again, Sharky's Machine, I'm Gonna Get You Sucka, Revenge of the Nerds,* and *Swamp Thing.*

8. FRED WILLIAMSON

Fred "The Hammer" Williamson was a hard-hitting cornerback who played for Pittsburgh, Oakland, and Kansas City between 1960 and 1967. His best year was 1962 when he intercepted eight passes for the Oakland Raiders. The Hammer has been seen in numerous films, including *M*A*S*H, Two Minute Warning,* and *The Longest Yard.*

9. JOE NAMATH

Broadway Joe Namath threw 173 touchdown passes during his Hall of Fame career, which spanned from 1965 until 1977. He led his New York Jets to a 16–7 upset victory over the Baltimore Colts in Super Bowl III. The highlight of his brief film career was a starring role opposite Ann-Margret in *C.C. and Company.*

10. MIKE HENRY

Linebacker Mike Henry played for the Pittsburgh Steelers and Los Angeles Rams from 1954 to 1964. He finished his career with nine interceptions. During the 1960s, Henry starred as Tarzan in the films *Tarzan and the Valley of Gold* and *Tarzan and the Jungle Boy.*

MADE FOR TV

From Monday Night Football to the Super Bowl, football has become the most popular sport on television. Some football stars have made their own mark on the small screen. Chicago Bears linebacking great Dick Butkus has made appearances on television programs ranging from *Magnum P.I.* to *Murder, She Wrote.* Baltimore's towering defensive lineman Bubba Smith played Robin, the night manager, in the 1981 sitcom, *Open All Night.* Years before he starred as himself in the long-running series, *The Adventures of Ozzie and Harriet,* Ozzie Nelson played football for Rutgers in 1926.

1. BILL COSBY

In 1961, Bill Cosby averaged 3.5 yards per carry in 36 rushing attempts for the Temple Owls. For three consecutive years beginning in 1965, Cosby won the Emmy for best actor in a drama series for his portrayal of undercover agent Alexander Scott in *I Spy. The Cosby Show,* which debuted in 1984, helped revitalize the situation comedy and was the number-one-rated television program for four consecutive years.

Temple University

Bill Cosby

Prior to his Emmy-winning role as Alexander Scott in *I Spy,* before his humorous Jell-O Pudding commercials, and long before his hugely popular sit-com *The Cosby Show,* Bill Cosby was a running back for the Temple University Owls.

2. WARD BOND

Ward Bond played on the 1930 Rose Bowl champion Southern California Trojans, a team known as the Thundering Herd. One of Hollywood's most successful character actors, Bond appeared in a string of classic films: *The Maltese Falcon, It's a Wonderful Life,* and *The Searchers,* to name just a few. His most famous role, however, was as Major Seth Adams on the top-rated television western, *Wagon Train.*

3. MERLIN OLSEN

As a member of the Los Angeles Rams' defensive line, the Fearsome Foursome, tackle Merlin Olsen played in a record 14 consecutive Pro Bowls. From 1977 to 1981, Olsen portrayed farmer Jonathan Garvey on the popular *Little House on the Prairie.* Olsen played the title role of Farmer Murphy in the 1981 series. He also starred in the short-lived Amish drama, *Aaron's Way,* in 1988, and hosted *Fantastic Facts* in 1991.

4. FRED DRYER

Fred Dryer was an outstanding defensive end for the Los Angeles Rams and New York Giants from 1969 to 1981. A Pro Bowler in 1976, Dryer is the only player in NFL history to record two safeties in one game, a feat he achieved on October 21, 1973. Dryer starred as Sergeant Rick Hunter in the police drama, *Hunter,* from 1984 to 1991. In 1995, Dryer played private eye Mike Land in the syndicated program, *Land's End.*

5. ED MARINARO

Cornell running back Ed Marinaro finished runner-up in the Heisman Trophy balloting in 1971. During his six-year professional career with the Minnesota Vikings, New York Jets, and Seattle Seahawks, Marinaro rushed for 1,319 yards and scored 13 touchdowns. For one season he played apartment manager Sonny St. Jacques in the hit sitcom, *Laverne and Shirley.* From 1981 through 1986, Marinaro starred as Officer Joe Coffey in the critically acclaimed police drama, *Hill Street Blues.* He also was a regular on the drama series, *Sisters,* from 1991 to 1994.

6. ALEX KARRAS

Detroit Lions' defensive tackle Alex Karras played from 1958 to 1970 and was a four-time Pro Bowler. Karras has appeared in many films, including *Paper Lion, Against All Odds,* and *Blazing Saddles,* in which he punched a horse. During the mid-1970s, Karras teamed with Howard Cosell and Frank Gifford on *Monday Night Football.* In 1975, he co-starred with wife, Susan Clark, in the TV movie *Babe,* based on the life of Babe Zaharias. His most notable television role was as ex-football player George Papadopolis in the popular sitcom *Webster,* which aired from 1983 to 1988.

7. MARK HARMON

The son of football great Tom Harmon, Mark Harmon played quarterback for UCLA. Harmon has been a regular on several television programs: *Sam, 240-Robert, Flamingo Road, Moonlighting, Reasonable Doubts,* and *Charlie Grace.* He played Dr. Bob Calswell on the medical drama *St. Elsewhere* from 1983 to 1986. He also turned in a strong performance as serial killer Ted Bundy in the made-for-TV movie *The Deliberate Stranger.*

8. LEE MAJORS

Lee Majors played football at Eastern Kentucky University in 1963. Majors starred in three long-running series. During the late 1960s, he portrayed Heath Barkley on *The Big Valley.* He played bionic man Steve Austin on the seventies drama, *The Six-Million Dollar Man.* Majors starred as stunt man Colt Seavers in *The Fall Guy,* a series which aired from 1981 to 1986.

9. JACK GING

Halfback Jack Ging played for Oklahoma in their 7–0 victory over Maryland in the 1954 Orange Bowl. Ging scored five touchdowns for the Sooners during his career. He starred as clinical psychologist Dr. Paul Graham in the medical drama *The Eleventh Hour,* a show that was on the air from 1962 to 1964. Ging also appeared in the television series *Wells Fargo* and *Riptide.*

10. HERMAN WEDEMEYER

An All-American halfback at St. Mary's College, Herman Wedemeyer played two seasons in the All-America Football Conference. The Hawaiian-born actor portrayed detective Duke Lakela on the police drama *Hawaii Five-O* from 1972 to 1980.

PLAYING POLITICS

Over the years dozens of individuals who played college or professional football have gone into politics. Lavern Dilweg, who played end for Green Bay between 1926 and 1934, was elected to Congress and served as an official in the Kennedy administration. Hall of Fame defensive back Yale Lary of the Detroit Lions was elected to the Texas legislature in 1958 while he was still active as a player.

Among the many past governors who played college football are George Carlson (Colorado), Earle Clements (Kentucky), William Gardiner (Maine), Bibb Graves (Alabama), Harry Leslie (Indiana), Leon Phillips (Oklahoma), Gifford Pinchot (Pennsylvania), R.G. Pleasant (Louisiana), Carl Sanders (Georgia), and Eugene Talmadge (Georgia).

It has become an annual tradition for presidents to phone their congratulations to Super Bowl winners, but not every president was a fan. When Calvin Coolidge was introduced to Red Grange of the Chicago Bears, he replied, "Nice to meet you, young man, I've always enjoyed animal acts." Here are some players who threw their helmets into the political ring.

1. GERALD FORD

Gerald Ford was the starting center for the University of Michigan from 1932 to 1934. He played in the 1935 College All-Star Game against the NFL champions, the Chicago Bears. He was such a great player that in 1959, he was selected to the *Sports Illustrated* Silver Anniversary All-American Team. While he attended law school, Ford coached football at Yale. He served 24 years in the U.S. House of Representatives and was named vice president in 1973. When Richard Nixon resigned in 1974, Gerald Ford became president of the United States.

2. DWIGHT EISENHOWER

Nickamed the "Kansas Cyclone," Dwight Eisenhower played halfback for Army in 1912. On November 9, 1912, Eisenhower was matched against the greatest running back of the day, Jim Thorpe of Carlisle. Army lost the game 27–6, and the next week Eisenhower suffered a knee injury in a game against Tufts. When he reinjured his knee vaulting a horse, Eisenhower's playing days were over. After a remarkable military career, which culminated with his success as the supreme Allied commander of the European theater during World War II, Eisenhower served two terms as president of the United States from 1953 to 1961.

3. JACK KEMP

Quarterback Jack Kemp played for the Steelers, Chargers, and Bills between 1957 and 1969. A brilliant field general, Kemp led Buffalo to American Football League championships in 1964 and 1965. He finished his pro career with 21,218 passing yards and threw 114 touchdown passes. In 1971, Kemp was elected to Congress representing New York's 31st district. Eighteen years later, he was appointed Secretary of the Department of Housing and Urban Development by President George Bush. Kemp was the Republican vice presidential candidate in the 1996 presidential election. He joked, "Pro football gave me a good sense of perspective to enter politics. I've already been booed, cheered, cut, sold, traded, and hung in effigy."

4. STEVE LARGENT

As a wide receiver for the Seattle Seahawks between 1976 and 1989, Steve Largent was known for his ability to deceive cornerbacks attempting to cover him. Raiders' defensive back Lester Hayes called him "The Master of Tomfoolery." During his playing days he set career records for most pass receptions (819), most receiving yards (13,089), and most touchdown receptions (100). He caught passes in an incredible 177 consecutive games. His career records have since been broken by the legendary Jerry Rice. In 1994, Largent was elected to the U.S. House of Representatives for a district in Oklahoma.

5. J.C. WATTS

Quarterback J.C. Watts led Oklahoma to a come-from-behind 18–17 victory over Florida State in the 1981 Orange Bowl. As the only African-American Republican in the House of Representatives, Watts is considered a rising star in national politics.

6. TED KENNEDY

Ted Kennedy played end for Harvard in 1955 and caught a touchdown pass versus Columbia. On November 19, 1955, he caught a seven-yard pass for his team's only touchdown in a 21–7 loss against arch rival Yale. A Massachusetts Democrat, Kennedy was elected to the U.S. Senate in 1962 and has served there ever since.

7. RICHARD NIXON

Richard Nixon may have not been the greatest football talent, but it wasn't for lack of trying. Nixon, a strapping 150-pounder, played on the freshman football team at Whittier College in 1930 because only eleven students tried out. He played on a freshman basketball team that did not win a game. On the varsity football team, Nixon, a tackle, saw action only in the last few minutes of a game, after the outcome was decided. A teammate recalled that Nixon was so eager that he was called offside on nearly every play. Despite his lack of success, Nixon once said, "My happiest moments of those college days involve sports." He admitted that he admired his football coach, Wallace "Chief" Newman, more than any other man except his father. He told Nixon, "Show me a good loser and I'll show you a loser." Nixon obviously remembered this advice in his famous "You won't have Nixon to kick around anymore" speech following his 1962 defeat for the California governorship. It was a rare defeat in a political career which saw him elected U.S. representative, U.S. Senator, vice president on the Eisenhower ticket, and in 1968, president of the United States.

8. RONALD REAGAN

Ronald Reagan was a member of the Eureka College football team. His most lasting contribution to football was his performance as the tragic Notre Dame star George Gipp in the 1940 movie, *Knute Rockne, All American.* Reagan was later elected governor of California, and he served two terms as president of the United States.

9. HAMILTON FISH

An All-American defensive standout, Hamilton Fish played tackle for Harvard in 1908 and 1909. The son of a U.S. congressman, Fish served 26 years in the House beginning in 1919. He chaired the first committee that investigated the threat of communism in America.

10. ENDICOTT PEABODY

Endicott "Chub" Peabody was an All-American guard at Harvard in 1941. Peabody served as governor of Massachusetts from 1963 to 1965.

COVERING ALL BASES

Many athletes have excelled at both football and baseball. Chuck Dressen is the only man to play pro football, major league baseball, and manage a major league team. Pro Football Hall of Famer Ace Parker homered in his first major league at-bat in 1937. Charlie Moran coached Centre College to their famous 1921 upset of Harvard, played major league baseball, and was a big-league umpire for 21 years. The 1953 Heisman runner-up, Paul Giel, won 11 games as a pitcher in the major leagues. Mississippi quarterback Jake Gibbs, who finished third in the 1960 Heisman voting, played ten years as a major-league catcher. University of Missouri quarterback Phil Bradley, the Big Eight total offense leader from 1978 to 1980, hit 26 home runs as an outfielder with the Seattle Mariners in 1985. Sam Chapman, an All-American running back at California, played in the 1938 Rose Bowl and in the 1946 baseball All-Star Game. Chuck Essegian played in the 1951 Rose Bowl as a Stanford linebacker and hit two homers in the 1959 World Series for the Los Angeles Dodgers. Alvin Dark, who had 2,089 hits in the majors, was such an outstanding runner at Louisiana State University that the great Steve Van Buren was his blocking back.

Other two-sport stars included Ransom Jackson, Harry Agganis, Morris Badgro, Paddy Driscoll, Charlie Berry, Tom Brown, Galen Cisco, Steve Garvey, Ted Kluszewski, John Stearns, Snuffy Stirnweiss, and Red Wilson.

1. CAL HUBBARD

Cal Hubbard holds the distinction of being the only man in the college, pro football, and baseball halls of fame. A pro football tackle from 1927 to 1935, he was selected to the NFL all-time team in 1969. Hubbard, a major-league umpire from 1936 to 1951, was elected to the Baseball Hall of Fame in 1976.

2. JIM THORPE

Often referred to as the greatest all-around athlete, Jim Thorpe hit .327 in his final major-league season in 1919. A star halfback from 1920 to 1928, Thorpe was elected to the Pro Football Hall of Fame in 1963.

3. BO JACKSON

Bo Jackson, a running back from Auburn University, won the 1985 Heisman Trophy. His four-year pro football career with the Los Angeles Raiders was highlighted by two 90-yard touchdown runs. A power-hitting outfielder with the Kansas City Royals, Jackson belted 32 home runs in 1989. He played in the 1989 All-Star Game and the 1990 NFL Pro Bowl.

4. JACKIE JENSEN

A 1,000-yard rusher with the University of California, Jackie Jensen finished fourth in the 1948 Heisman Trophy balloting. He ran for a 67-yard touchdown in the 1949 Rose Bowl against Northwestern. An all-star outfielder with the Boston Red Sox, Jensen three times led the league in runs batted in and was the 1958 American League Most Valuable Player.

5. DEION SANDERS

One of the greatest cornerbacks in NFL history, Deion Sanders played on Super Bowl championship teams with the Dallas Cowboys and San Francisco Forty-Niners. "Neon Deion," as he is sometimes called, was also voted the NFL defensive player of the year in 1994. A fleet outfielder with the Yankees, Giants, Braves, and Reds, Sanders batted .304 and led the National League with 14 triples in 1992 for Atlanta.

6. JACKIE ROBINSON

Jackie Robinson averaged 11.4 yards per rush and intercepted four passes for UCLA in 1939. He scored on a 46-yard touchdown pass in the 1941 College All-Star Game against the world champion Chicago Bears. In 1947, Robinson broke baseball's color barrier and batted .311 during his ten-year major-league career. Robinson was voted the greatest second baseman in major-league history by fans in 1999.

7. ERNIE NEVERS

A member of both the college and pro football halls of fame, Ernie Nevers scored 40 points for the Chicago Cardinals in a game against the Chicago Bears in 1929, a record that still stands. Nevers won six games as a pitcher in the major leagues with the St. Louis Browns and gave up two home runs to Babe Ruth during the Bambino's historic 60-home-run season in 1927.

8. GEORGE HALAS

George Halas played 12 games with the New York Yankees in 1919 before he hurt his leg sliding. A founder of the National Football League in 1920, Halas coached the Chicago Bears to 325 wins and six NFL championships.

9. VIC JANOWICZ

Ohio State halfback Vic Janowicz was the 1950 Heisman Trophy winner. He spent two seasons with the Pittsburgh Pirates, batting .214 in 83 games. Janowicz scored seven touchdowns in two seasons with the Washington Redskins before an automobile accident in 1956 ended his career.

10. GREASY NEALE

Earle "Greasy" Neale played eight seasons as an outfielder in the major leagues. A member of the 1919 world champion Cincinnati Reds, Neale coached the Philadelphia Eagles to NFL titles in both 1948 and 1949 and was elected to the Pro Football Hall of Fame.

BASKET CASES

John Havlicek, a basketball star at Ohio State, was selected by the Cleveland Browns in the seventh round of the 1962 NFL draft. He played wide receiver in one exhibition game before being cut. Havlicek scored more than 26,000 points in sixteen seasons with the Boston Celtics. Kentucky basketball standout Pat Riley was selected in the eleventh round of the 1967 NFL draft by the Dallas Cowboys. Opting for pro basketball, Riley played nine seasons before coaching the Los Angeles Lakers to several NBA titles. Unlike Havlicek and Riley, the following athletes succeeded in both football and basketball.

1. **CHARLIE WARD**

Florida State quarterback Charlie Ward was a runaway winner of the 1993 Heisman Trophy. Instead of playing professional football, Ward became a point guard with the NBA New York Knicks.

2. **OTTO GRAHAM**

Otto Graham quarterbacked the Cleveland Browns for ten seasons between 1946 and 1955. The Browns reached the

Jon SooHoo

Charlie Ward

Because of questions about his size and arm strength, quarterback Charlie Ward was not drafted by an NFL team despite winning the Heisman Trophy.

championship game all ten years, winning seven of them. Their record with Graham at quarterback was 105–17–4. An All-American basketball player at Northwestern, Graham averaged 5.2 points a game for the Rochester Royals during the 1945–1946 season.

3. **BUD GRANT**

Bud Grant played forward for two seasons with the Minneapolis Lakers, averaging 2.6 points per game. He was a member of the 1950 NBA champions. Turning to pro football, he caught 56 passes for 997 yards and seven touchdowns with the Philadelphia Eagles in 1952. His greatest fame came as coach of the Minnesota Vikings. Grant led the Vikings to four Super Bowl appearances, earning himself a spot in the Pro Football Hall of Fame.

4. **LONNIE WRIGHT**

A defensive back for the Denver Broncos in 1966 and 1967, Lonnie Wright intercepted five passes. Wright played five seasons in the American Basketball Association with Denver and Florida. During the 1968–1969 season, the guard averaged 16.4 points per game.

5. **OTTO SCHNELLBACHER**

During the 1948–1949 season, Otto Schnellbacher averaged 6.4 points playing for the Providence Steamrollers and St. Louis Bombers of the Basketball Association of America. In only four seasons as a defensive back, Schnellbacher intercepted 34 passes for New York teams in the All-America Football Conference and National Football League.

6. RON WIDBY

Ron Widby scored 2.9 points per game with New Orleans of the American Basketball Association during the 1967–1968 season. Widby spent six seasons as a punter for the Cowboys and Packers and played for Dallas in Super Bowl V.

7. K.C. JONES

K.C. Jones played guard on two consecutive NCAA basketball championship teams with the University of San Francisco. Although he never played college football, Jones was drafted in the 30th round of the NFL draft by the Los Angeles Rams. During training camp, Jones, a cornerback, tried a defense based on the full-court press he used in basketball. It was an early version of the bump-and-run coverage. Jones joined the Boston Celtics and was an integral part of eight consecutive NBA championship teams.

8. HANK SOAR

Hank Soar played fullback, quarterback, and defensive back for the New York Giants from 1937 to 1946. Soar played in four NFL championship games. He coached Providence of the NBA during the 1947–1948 season. Soar also umpired in the American League from 1953 to 1973.

9. TERRY BAKER

Oregon State quarterback Terry Baker won the 1962 Heisman Trophy. His 99-yard touchdown run gave his team a 6–0 victory over Villanova in the Liberty Bowl. Baker was a starting guard on Oregon State's 1963 Final Four basketball team.

10. DUTCH CLARK

Tailback Dutch Clark played in the National Football League from 1931 to 1938. Four times he led the league in rushing touchdowns. On December 18, 1932, Clark, the star runner for Portsmouth, chose to miss the NFL championship game against Chicago in order to coach the Colorado College basketball team. Without Clark, Portsmouth lost the game, 9–0.

GOING FOR THE GOLD

Olympic medalists frequently parlay their success into NFL careers. Pete Mehringer (Kansas University), the light heavyweight freestyle wrestling gold medalist at the 1932 Olympics, played tackle and guard for the Chicago Bears from 1934 to 1936. The 1932 decathlon champion, Jim Bausch (Kansas University), played tailback, defensive back, and linebacker for Chicago and Cincinnati in 1933. Glenn Morris (Colorado State), the 1936 decathlon gold medalist, played end for the 1940 Detroit Lions. Henry Carr (Arizona State), who won gold in the 200-meter dash at the 1964 Olympics, intercepted seven passes as a defensive back for the New York Giants from 1965 to 1967. Tommie Smith (San Jose State), the 1968 200-meter champion, played two games as a wide receiver for the 1969 Cincinnati Bengals. Jim Hines (Texas Southern), the 1968 gold medalist in the 100-meter dash, played wide receiver for the Miami Dolphins and Kansas City Chiefs in 1969 and 1970. Gerald Tinker (Kent State), a gold medalist in the 400-meter relay at the 1972 Olympics, played wide receiver for the Atlanta Falcons and Green Bay Packers in 1974 and 1975.

1. JIM THORPE

Jim Thorpe, a gold medalist in both the decathlon and pentathlon at the 1912 Stockholm Olympics, played eight seasons of professional football. One of the greatest track-and-field athletes of all time, Thorpe also ranks among football's immortals.

2. BOB HAYES

Known as the world's fastest human, Bullet Bob Hayes won the gold medal in the 100-meter dash at the 1964 Tokyo Olympics. During his NFL career, which lasted from 1965 to 1975, Hayes caught 371 passes and scored 76 touchdowns.

3. OLLIE MATSON

Ollie Matson won a bronze medal in the 400-meter dash and a silver medal in the 1,600-meter relay at the 1952 Olympics. An outstanding NFL running back from 1952 until 1966, Matson rushed for 5,173 yards and scored 73 touchdowns. He was elected to the Pro Football Hall of Fame in 1972.

4. BO ROBERSON

The silver medalist in the long jump at the 1960 Rome Olympics, Bo Roberson played wide receiver and halfback in the American Football League from 1961 to 1966. Roberson finished his career with 176 receptions and scored 19 touchdowns.

5. RON BROWN

A gold medalist in the 4x100-meter relay at the 1984 Los Angeles Olympics, Ron Brown used his speed to become a feared wide receiver and kickoff returner in the National Football League. Brown played for the Los Angeles Rams from 1984 to 1991 and caught 98 passes, including 13 for touchdowns. In 1985, he led the league, averaging 32.7 yards per kickoff return, and ran back three for touchdowns.

6. JOHNNY LAM JONES

Johnny Lam Jones won a gold medal as a member of the 1976 4x100-meter relay team. Jones played wide receiver for the New York Jets from 1980 to 1984. His best season was 1983, when he caught 43 passes for 734 yards.

7. MICHAEL CARTER

Michael Carter played his first professional football game six days after taking home the silver medal in the shotput at the 1984 Olympics. Carter played defensive tackle for nine seasons for the San Francisco Forty-Niners.

8. BOB MATHIAS

The decathlon champion at both the 1948 and 1952 Olympics, Bob Mathias played fullback for Stanford in the 1952 Rose Bowl against Illinois. The high point of Mathias' football career was a 96-yard kickoff return versus the University of Southern California.

9. GLENN DAVIS

Glenn Davis won gold medals in the 400-meter hurdles at both the 1956 and 1960 Olympics. Davis caught ten passes during his two seasons as a wide receiver with the Detroit Lions.

10. MILT CAMPBELL

Milt Campbell upset Rafer Johnson to win the gold medal in the decathlon at the 1956 Olympics. Campbell played halfback for the Cleveland Browns in 1957 and caught one pass for a 25-yard touchdown.

GRIDIRON GRAPPLERS

For almost as long as professional football has been in existence, players have gone into pro wrestling. Lex Luger, a two-time WCW World Champion, was an offensive lineman with Montreal in the Canadian Football League and earned a tryout with the Green Bay Packers. Linebacker Kevin Greene, who ranks among the NFL's all-time sack leaders, teamed with wrestling greats Roddy Piper and Ric Flair to win a six-man tag-team event at the 1997 pay-per-view Slamboree. That same night, all-time sack leader Reggie White lost to Steve McMichael in another wrestling bout. In 1995, Lawrence Taylor, often called the greatest defensive player in NFL history, defeated wrestling behemoth Bam Bam Bigelow at Wrestlemania XI. During the peak of his career, Baltimore defensive lineman Gene "Big Daddy" Lipscomb earned three times more money wrestling than playing football. Other football stars who climbed into the wrestling ring included Brian Pillman, Alex Karras, Jim Covert, Bill Fralic, Russ Francis, Ernie Holmes, Harvey Martin, William Perry, Mark Gastineau, Walter Johnson, Ron Pritchard, and Leo Nomellini.

1. DICK THE BRUISER

An offensive lineman for the Green Bay Packers from 1951 to 1954, Dick Afflis once broke the leg of a Chicago Bears player during a game. In the wrestling ring, Dick the Bruiser earned his reputation as the "world's most dangerous wrestler." In November 1966, he reached the pinnacle of his sport by winning the AWA world title from Mad Dog Vachon. The Bruiser teamed up with The Crusher to win the world tag-team title five times.

2. BRONKO NAGURSKI

Bronko Nagurski is the only member of the Pro Football Hall of Fame to win a wrestling world title. In 1939, Nagurski defeated the legendary Lou Thesz to win the National Wrestling Alliance belt. Nagurski won the title for a second time in 1941. His trademark wrestling move was a flying block.

3. BILL GOLDBERG

Perhaps no wrestler ever had a more spectacular beginning to a career than Bill Goldberg. A two-time All Southeast Conference selection, Goldberg had 348 tackles during his college career at Georgia. The nose tackle played with the Atlanta Falcons from 1992 to 1994. He won the WCW World Wrestling championship from Hulk Hogan in July 1998. Goldberg amassed a 173-match winning streak before finally losing to Kevin Nash.

4. THE ROCK

Duane Johnson, known in the ring as "The Rock," was a defensive lineman for the University of Miami in the early 1990s. The son of former tag-team champion Rocky Johnson, he played one season with the Calgary Stampeders of the Canadian Football League before turning to professional wrestling full time. With catch phrases such as "Smell what The Rock is cooking," he quickly became a fan favorite. The Rock won the World Wrestling Federation (WWF) championship for the first time on November 15, 1998, with a victory over Mankind. His popularity is so great that his book, *The Rock Says,* became a bestseller, and he hosted *Saturday Night Live.*

5. GUS SONNENBERG

A four-time All-Pro tackle, Gus Sonnenberg defeated the immortal Ed "Strangler" Lewis for the National Wrestling Alliance world title on January 4, 1929. Despite being only five-foot, five-inches tall and weighing only 195 pounds, Sonnenberg defeated Lewis in four of their five matches. His trademark move was the flying tackle. Sonnenberg made over a million dollars wrestling before he was forced to retire in 1939 with an irregular heartbeat.

6. RON SIMMONS

Ron Simmons was an All-American nose guard at Florida State in 1979 and 1980. In August 1992, he became the first African-American wrestling champion when he defeated Vader for the National Wrestling Alliance world championship. In recent years he has enjoyed success in the WWF as Faarooq.

7. STEVE AUSTIN

"Stone Cold" Steve Austin is probably the most popular wrestler since the heyday of Hulk Hogan. At North Texas State University, defensive tackle Steve Anderson made 55 tackles and had four sacks in his senior year. Changing his name to Steve Austin, in honor of the Six Million Dollar Man, he defeated Shawn Michaels on April 28, 1998, to win the WWF title. The referee for the Wrestlemania XIV bout was former heavyweight boxing champion Mike Tyson.

8. WAHOO MCDANIEL

Wahoo McDaniel played football for the University of Oklahoma from 1956 to 1960. He spent nine seasons in pro football, playing linebacker for the Houston Oilers, Denver Broncos, New York Jets, and Miami Dolphins. The two-time All Pro intercepted 13 passes during his career. McDaniel won the United States Wrestling title four times between 1981 and 1984.

9. ERNIE LADD

Ernie "The Cat" Ladd played defensive tackle for San Diego, Houston, and Kansas City from 1961 to 1968. Ladd was All Pro in 1964 and 1965. The self-proclaimed "King of Wrestling," he was the North American Heavyweight Wrestling Champion in the 1970s. The six-foot, nine-inch, 315-pound Ladd carried on a feud with Andre the Giant.

10. STEVE McMICHAEL

Steve "Mongo" McMichael played defensive tackle in the NFL from 1980 to 1994. He was a member of the Super Bowl champion Chicago Bears in 1985. The highlight of McMichael's wrestling career was winning the United States title in August 1997.

INTELLECTUAL ASSASSINS

Joe Theismann said, "The word 'genius' isn't applicable in football. A genius is a guy like Norman Einstein." A few players have proven him wrong. Dan Fortmann, a Phi Beta Kappa graduate of Colgate, played guard and linebacker for the Chicago Bears from 1936 to 1945 before pursuing a medical degree. Harlan Stone, the Chief Justice of the United States Supreme Court from 1941 to 1946, played football at Amherst in 1893.

1. WHIZZER WHITE

Byron "Whizzer" White, a halfback for the University of Colorado, finished second in the 1937 Heisman Trophy balloting. In the 1938 Cotton Bowl against Rice, White caught a touchdown pass and ran back an interception 47 yards for another score.

A true scholar athlete, he was also the university's valedictorian. A first-round draft choice by Pittsburgh, White led the NFL in rushing during his rookie season in 1938. He was paid the league's first five-figure salary, $15,800 a year. White accepted a Rhodes scholarship and missed the entire 1939 season. A year later, White again led the NFL in rushing, this time with the Detroit Lions. He retired from football in 1941. In 1961, White was named deputy attorney general of the United States and the following year was appointed an associate justice of the United States Supreme Court by President Kennedy.

2. PAUL ROBESON

Paul Robeson was a man of many talents. One of the first African-Americans to attend Rutgers University, Robeson was a two-time All American in football and a Phi Beta Kappa student. Robeson scored two touchdowns during his two seasons in professional football. In 1923, he received his law degree from Columbia University. An outstanding actor, he starred in many critically acclaimed productions, including *Porgy, The Hairy Ape,* and *Othello.* He used his magnificent bass-baritone voice memorably in the musical *Showboat.*

3. PETE DAWKINS

The Heisman Trophy winner in 1958, halfback Pete Dawkins of Army graduated seventh in his class at West Point. A Rhodes scholar, Dawkins did not pursue a career in professional football. In 1983, the 45-year-old Dawkins became the youngest general in the army.

4. DICK KAZMAIER

A cum laude graduate of Princeton, tailback Dick Kazmaier won the Heisman Trophy in 1951. Rather than play professional football, Kazmaier established his own marketing and financial services businesses.

5. JIMMY CONZELMAN

Jimmy Conzelman scored 26 touchdowns during his professional football career, which lasted from 1920 until 1929. In 1928, he coached Providence to an NFL title and nineteen years later led the Chicago Cardinals to a championship. The Hall of Famer also had careers as a major-league baseball executive, newspaper publisher, playwright, songwriter, and actor.

6. BILL CORBUS

Bill "The Baby-Faced Assassin" Corbus was an All-American guard for Stanford in 1932 and 1933. Corbus was president of the student body and a magna cum laude graduate. Years later he became a vice president in the A&P supermarket chain.

7. CLIFF BATTLES

Cliff Battles was a Phi Beta Kappa scholar at West Virginia Wesleyan. During his Hall of Fame pro career, Battles led the National Football League in rushing in 1932 and 1937.

8. JOHNNY BLOOD

An all-purpose back during his NFL career, which lasted from 1925 to 1938, Johnny Blood scored 49 touchdowns. While attending Notre Dame, he admitted that he wrote the English compositions for Harry Stuhldreher, one of the famed Four Horsemen. Blood could recite by memory the work of many poets and once challenged actor John Barrymore to a Shakespeare reciting contest in a Pittsburgh bar. Blood also had a strong interest in economics.

9. GEORGE KUNZ

On the field, George Kunz was an All-American offensive tackle at Notre Dame. In the classroom, he was a cum laude graduate who majored in philosophy. Kunz was the recipient of the prestigious Scholar Athlete Award at the university. In the pros, Kunz was an eight-time Pro Bowler.

10. **Ron Mix**

Offensive lineman Ron Mix, an All-American Football League selection from 1960 to 1968, was known as the "Intellectual Assassin" because of his combination of brain and brawn. After his playing days were over, Mix became an attorney.

PAPER LIONS

Players named Russ Reader and Bill Story have played in the NFL, but football has stronger literary ties.

1. TIM GREEN

A defensive end for the Atlanta Falcons from 1986 to 1993, Tim Green recorded 24 career sacks. After he retired from football, Green wrote several novels: *Ruffians, Titans, Outlaws,* and *Marauders.* His book *The Dark Side of the Game* was an exposé of the violence and drugs which are prevalent in professional football.

2. GEORGE PLIMPTON

George Plimpton is best known as an author and publisher of a literary magazine, *The Paris Review.* In 1966, Plimpton published a bestseller, *Paper Lion,* about his tryout at quarterback with the Detroit Lions. Two years later it was made into a movie with Alan Alda playing Plimpton and Lions' defensive tackle Alex Karras as himself.

3. PETE GENT

Receiver Pete Gent caught 68 passes for the Dallas Cowboys between 1964 and 1968. Five years after he retired from the game, Gent published a novel, *North Dallas Forty.* The book was one of the first to give a behind-the-scenes account of professional football.

4. JACK KEROUAC

Jack Kerouac was such a good football player at Lowell High School in Massachusetts that he attracted the attention of college scouts from Duke, Boston College, and Columbia. Kerouac accepted an athletic scholarship at Columbia. In his second game as a freshman, he dazzled onlookers with a 90-yard kickoff return for a touchdown. A few plays later, as Kerouac returned a punt, he was tackled and suffered a broken leg. Once his football career was over, he turned his attention to literature. His novel *On the Road,* published in 1957, was a literary landmark and made Kerouac a leader of the Beat movement.

5. F. SCOTT FITZGERALD

Although he was five-foot, seven-inches tall and weighed less than 140 pounds, F. Scott Fitzgerald had dreams of becoming a football star. He played quarterback at Newman Prep and was known mainly for his injuries. Once he broke a rib and on another occasion was bedridden after he tackled a larger player. When he dropped a pass that cost his team a victory, Fitzgerald burst into tears. Notified that he had been accepted at Princeton University, he wired his mother, "Please send my football pads and shoes immediately." An ankle injury ended his football career at Princeton after only three days. He proved much more successful at writing, and his 1925 book, *The Great Gatsby,* is considered one of the finest American novels.

6. EDGAR ALLAN POE

Football didn't even exist during the life of author Edgar Allan Poe (1809–1849). However, his descendents left their mark on the game. Five of Poe's great nephews played football at Princeton between 1880 and 1896—Samuel, Arthur, John, Edgar Allan, and Neilson. His namesake, Edgar Allan Poe, was the quarterback on the first All-American team in 1889.

7. JAMES DICKEY

Renowned poet and novelist James Dickey played football for Clemson University in 1941. A winner of the National Book Award, Dickey's most famous novel was *Deliverance.*

8. ARCHIBALD MACLEISH

Before he became one of the most acclaimed poets of the twentieth century, Archibald Macleish played football for Yale in 1913. His literary awards include two Pulitzer Prizes for poetry and one for drama. Macleish was the librarian of Congress from 1939 to 1944 and president of the American Academy of Arts and Letters.

9. JOHN HERSEY

John Hersey played football at Yale University, from which he graduated in 1935. Hersey is best remembered for his war novels. His book *A Bell for Adano,* dealing with the occupation of Sicily during World War II, won the Pulitzer Prize for fiction in 1945.

10. JOHN F. KENNEDY

Future president John F. Kennedy played football for the junior varsity at Harvard in 1939. Kennedy's college thesis was turned into the book *Why England Slept. Profiles in Courage,* published in 1956, earned him a Pulitzer Prize.

SLIPPERY ROCK AND WALLA WALLA

More than 400 athletes who played college football at Notre Dame have gone on to the NFL. Major universities such as Ohio State, the University of Southern California, UCLA, and Michigan are also among the best proving grounds for professional football players. Surprisingly, a number of obscure colleges have produced NFL players. In some cases, these future NFL players spent only part of their college careers at these obscure schools before transferring to big-time programs. Some unlikely alma maters include the American College of Physical Education, Antelope Valley, Bemidji State, Bliss College, Charles Stewart Mott Community College, Christian Brothers, College of the Desert, Diablo Valley, Foothill College, General Motors Institute, Itawamba, Philander Smith, and Slippery Rock.

1. NAVARRO JUNIOR COLLEGE

Believe it or not, Navarro Junior College in Texas has had nearly two dozen of its alumni play professional football. The list is headed by fleet receiver Eddie Brown, who caught 363 passes for 41 touchdowns during his career with the

Cincinnati Bengals from 1985 to 1991. Following his days at Navarro Junior College, Brown played at the University of Miami.

2. HINDS

Hinds Community College in Mississippi has had 18 of its players see NFL action. Two Hinds alumni, Leon Lett of the Dallas Cowboys and John Copeland (who later transferred to the University of Alabama) of the Cincinnati Bengals were starters on their respective defensive lines throughout most of the 1990s. Lett, during his prime, was one of the league's premier defensive tackles.

3. FERRUM

Ferrum is a small college located in Ferrum, Virginia. Thirteen Ferrum students have gone on to play in the NFL. The most famous Ferrum alumnus is Chris Warren, a three-time All-Pro running back who rushed for nearly 7,000 yards with Seattle during the 1990s.

4. MORRIS BROWN

Morris Brown College of Atlanta, Georgia, has produced a dozen players who have played in the NFL. Defensive back Butch Atkinson intercepted 30 passes for the Raiders between 1968 and 1977. Wide receiver Alfred Jenkins made 360 receptions and scored 40 touchdowns for the Atlanta Falcons from 1975 to 1983.

5. RIPON

Eleven Ripon alumni have NFL experience. The Wisconsin college also holds the distinction of producing some of the most interesting names ever to appear on pro football rosters. Ripon graduates include Tiny Croft, Boob Darling, Tubby Howard, Champ Seibold, and Cowboy Wheeler.

6. NEW MEXICO MILITARY INSTITUTE

The New Mexico Military Institute may not be a household name, but eleven of its students have played in the NFL. The most notable is Roger Staubach, who went on to win the Heisman Trophy at Navy and lead the Dallas Cowboys to victory in Super Bowl VI.

7. BLINN COLLEGE

Eleven future NFL players attended Blinn Junior College in Texas. Lyle Blackwood played defensive back for Cincinnati, Seattle, Baltimore, and Miami between 1973 and 1986. In 1977, Blackwood, then with the Baltimore Colts, led the league in interceptions with ten.

8. WALLA WALLA

Walla Walla Community College in Washington State can boast ten alumni who have joined the NFL ranks. Kimo Van Oelhoffen was a starting defensive tackle for the Cincinnati Bengals in the late 1990s.

9. GUSTAVUS ADOLPHUS

Gustavus Adolphus, located in St. Peter, Minnesota, is not exactly a football mecca, but the school has eight NFL players to its credit. Tom Harmon attended Gustavus Adolphus prior to winning the Heisman Trophy in 1940 with Michigan and playing halfback in the NFL with the Los Angeles Rams.

10. SADDLEBACK

Saddleback Junior College in California has prepared eight players for NFL careers. Two Saddleback alumni went on to star with the Kansas City Chiefs: Quarterback Bill Kenney played for the Chiefs between 1980 and 1988 and led the NFL in completions in 1983. Wide receiver Stephone Paige caught 377 passes for Kansas City between 1983 and 1991.

WHAT MIGHT HAVE BEEN

Injuries are a part of football. During their careers, most players experience injuries that cause them to miss games. Some injuries are so serious that they hamper a player's performance or even end his career. The following gifted players had their careers shortened by injury, illness, or death.

1. ERNIE DAVIS

Ernie Davis had a tough act to follow at Syracuse. A few years earlier, Jim Brown had rewritten the Syracuse record book. But in 1961, Davis accomplished something not even the great Jim Brown had: The halfback became the first African-American to win the Heisman Trophy. Davis was preparing to play football for the Cleveland Browns when he was hospitalized in the summer of 1962. Diagnosed with leukemia, he never had the opportunity to play in a professional game. Ernie Davis died on May 18, 1963, at the age of 23.

2. GREG COOK

Few quarterbacks displayed the potential of Greg Cook. Known as the "Blond Bomber," Cook, playing at the University of Cincinnati, passed for more than 550 yards in a game against Ohio University. Drafted by the Cincinnati Bengals in the first round in 1969, Cook was an immediate sensation. He led the league in passing and averaged an incredible 9.41 yards per pass attempt. Unfortunately, he injured his shoulder during the season and had to endure three operations. Cook never regained his arm strength and threw only three more passes in his pro career.

3. GALE SAYERS

No player ever made more impact on the game in so short a time as running back Gale Sayers. As a rookie with the Chicago Bears in 1965, he scored 22 touchdowns. In a memorable game against the San Francisco Forty-Niners, Sayers scored six touchdowns, including two carries of more than 80 yards. The next season he led the NFL in rushing. In 1969, his last full season, Sayers captured a second rushing title. A series of knee injuries effectively brought his career to an end at age 26. Despite playing only four full seasons, Sayers' statistics are staggering. He averaged 5.0 yards per carry, 14.5 yards per punt return, and a record 30.6 yards per kickoff return.

4. WILLIAM ANDREWS

Although far less well known, Atlanta Falcons' running back William Andrews suffered a fate similar to Gale Sayers'. Andrews rushed for more than 1,000 yards in each of his first four full seasons. His best season was 1983, when he rushed for 1,567 yards, caught 59 passes, and scored 11 touchdowns. In 1984, Andrews tore up his knee and missed two seasons. His comeback in 1986 was unsuccessful, and Andrews scored only one more touchdown.

5. JOE DELANEY

During his rookie season in 1981, Kansas City Chiefs' running back Joe Delaney rushed for 1,121 yards. On June 29, 1983, the 24-year-old Delaney drowned while attempting to rescue children who had fallen into a pool in Monroe, Louisiana.

6. ICKEY WOODS

Elbert "Ickey" Woods gained 1,066 yards during his rookie season with the Cincinnati Bengals in 1988. Known for the "Ickey Shuffle," a dance he performed in the end zone following each touchdown, Woods had plenty of chances to dance as he scored 15 touchdowns that season and led Cincinnati to the Super Bowl. The following season, Woods injured his knee and was finished by age 25.

7. KI-JANA CARTER

Another Bengals' running back to suffer a devastating knee injury was Ki-Jana Carter. The Penn State alum finished second in the 1994 Heisman Trophy voting and was selected as the number one overall pick in the 1995 draft by Cincinnati. Everyone expected Carter to be a star for years. Those hopes were dashed when Carter injured his knee in the team's first exhibition game and missed the entire season. The next year, Carter was a disappointment, and by 1997 had lost his starting job to rookie back Corey Dillon.

8. JEFF BURKETT

Jeff Burkett was a rookie punter for the Chicago Cardinals in 1947. He was averaging 47.4 yards per punt when he was killed in a plane crash on October 24, 1947. The year's eventual punting leader, Jack Jacobs of Green Bay, averaged four yards fewer per punt for the season.

9. NILE KINNICK

Iowa halfback Nile Kinnick won the 1939 Heisman Trophy, outpolling Tom Harmon of Michigan. During World War II, Kinnick joined the navy. In June 1943, he was killed when his military aircraft crashed into the sea.

10. CALVIN JONES

Another ill-fated Iowa alumnus, guard Calvin Jones won the 1955 Outland Trophy as the nation's outstanding college lineman. In December 1956, Jones perished in an airplane crash near Vancouver, British Columbia.

HEISMAN BUSTS

The Heisman Trophy signifies excellence in college football. Heisman winners such as Paul Hornung, Roger Staubach, O.J. Simpson, Jim Plunkett, Tony Dorsett, Earl Campbell, Marcus Allen, and Barry Sanders have gone on to become professional superstars. Not every Heisman candidate has been so lucky. Here is a roster of Heisman busts.

1. RANDY DUNCAN

Iowa quarterback Randy Duncan finished second in the 1958 Heisman Trophy voting. The number-one pick in the 1959 draft by Green Bay, Duncan never played with the Packers. Two years later he saw his only pro action as a back-up quarterback with the Dallas Texans. Duncan completed only 37 percent of his passes and threw only one touchdown pass.

2. TERRY BAKER

The 1962 Heisman Trophy winner, quarterback Terry Baker of Oregon State, was drafted in the first round by the Los Angeles Rams. A back-up quarterback for three seasons, Baker finished his pro career with 12 completions, four interceptions, and zero touchdown passes.

3. JOE BELLINO

Joe Bellino of Navy was a runaway winner of the 1960 Heisman Trophy. After fulfilling his military obligations, the halfback signed with the Boston Patriots in 1965. The seldom-used Bellino played three years in Boston. He averaged only 2.1 yards per carry and did not score a touchdown.

4. JOHN HUARTE

Notre Dame quarterback John Huarte finished first in the 1964 Heisman Trophy balloting, ahead of future Bears great Dick Butkus. Drafted in the second round by the New York Jets, Huarte's career was doomed from the start. The Jets had used their first-round pick to select Alabama quarterback Joe Namath. Waived by the Jets, Huarte spent most of his seven-year career on the taxi squads of the Patriots, Eagles, Vikings, Chiefs, and Bears. Between 1966 and 1972, Huarte completed only 19 passes and threw only one touchdown pass.

5. GARY BEBAN

In 1967, UCLA quarterback Gary Beban outpolled USC running back O.J. Simpson to win the Heisman Trophy. While Simpson went on to NFL greatness, Beban struggled. Drafted by the Los Angeles Rams, he was traded to the Washington Redskins. For two seasons, Beban served as a back-up quarterback and running back. He never completed a pass in the NFL.

6. PAT SULLIVAN

Auburn quarterback Pat Sullivan led the country in total offense in 1970. The following year he won the Heisman Trophy. A second-round draft pick by the Atlanta Falcons, Sullivan spent four seasons as a reserve quarterback. For his career, Sullivan threw five touchdown passes and 16 interceptions.

7. CHUCK LONG

The 1985 Heisman voting was the closest on record as Auburn running back Bo Jackson edged Iowa quarterback Chuck Long for the award. Long was drafted in the first round by the Detroit Lions. In 1987, his only season as a starter, he threw for 11 touchdowns but was intercepted 20 times.

8. HEATH SHULER

Heath Shuler, a quarterback for the University of Tennessee, finished second in the 1993 Heisman voting. Considered a can't-miss prospect by many, Shuler was selected as the third pick overall by the Washington Redskins. Within a year, Shuler had lost his starting job to a seventh-round draft choice named Gus Frerotte.

9. GINO TORRETTA

Gino Torretta, the 1992 Heisman winner, played quarterback for the University of Miami. Drafted by the Vikings, he played only one game in Minnesota. Three years later Torretta appeared in one game for the Seattle Seahawks. Torretta completed five of 16 passes for only 41 yards.

10. ANDRE WARE

The 1989 Heisman winner was Andre Ware, quarterback for the University of Houston. The first-round pick of the Lions, Ware was a sporadic starter in his four seasons in Detroit.

DRAFT STEALS

In every draft there are players who slip through the cracks. It may be because they're too slow, or too small, or did not attend a major college. Dwight Clark, a tenth-round pick by San Francisco in 1979, caught 506 passes for the Forty-Niners between 1979 and 1987. His fingertip catch against Dallas in the fourth quarter of the 1982 NFL championship game sent the Forty-Niners to the Super Bowl. Defensive back Pat Fischer wasn't selected until the 17th round of the 1961 draft because scouts thought he was too small to play in the NFL. He proved them wrong by intercepting 56 passes during his 17-year career with St. Louis and Washington. Tom Sestak, a 17th-round pick by Buffalo in 1962, was a four-time all-AFL selection at defensive tackle. A 12th-round pick in the 1967 draft, running back Preston Pearson played in five Super Bowls for three different teams (Baltimore, Pittsburgh, and Dallas).

1. JOHNNY UNITAS

During his senior year at the University of Louisville, quarterback Johnny Unitas completed 44 out of 110 passes for

527 yards and only three touchdowns. As a result, he was not selected until the ninth round of the 1955 NFL draft by Pittsburgh. Steelers' coach Walt Kiesling cut Unitas because he thought he was too dumb to be an NFL quarterback. Instead of playing professional football, Unitas was paid six dollars a game to play for a semi-pro team in Bloomfield, New Jersey. The next season, the Baltimore Colts signed Unitas as a back-up quarterback to George Shaw, who had been the number-one pick in the 1955 draft. When Shaw broke his kneecap, Unitas stepped in and the rest is history. A ten-time Pro Bowler, Unitas threw 290 touchdown passes and is considered by many to be the greatest quarterback in NFL history. His record of 47 consecutive games in which he threw at least one touchdown pass may never be broken.

2. **BART STARR**

Bart Starr was so lightly regarded after his collegiate career at Alabama that the quarterback was not selected until the 17th round of the 1956 draft by Green Bay. The Packers' number-one pick that season, halfback Jack Losch, gained only 43 yards during his one season in Green Bay. By contrast, Starr spent 16 seasons as a Packer. When coach Vince Lombardi came to Green Bay in 1959, he was less than starstruck by his quarterback. His first choice for the starting job was Lamar McHan until McHan separated his shoulder. Lombardi's second choice, Joe Francis, was benched after the team lost five games in a row. Once Starr was inserted into the lineup, the Packers became a powerhouse. Starr led the Packers to five NFL championships and victories in the first two Super Bowls. A three-time NFL passing leader, Starr set a record by throwing 294 passes without an interception.

3. GEORGE BLANDA

Quarterback and place-kicker George Blanda was a 12th-round pick by the Chicago Bears in the 1949 NFL draft. For ten seasons, Blanda saw limited action as a quarterback. After the 1958 season, he retired because the Bears wanted to use him only as a kicker. In 1960, he got a second chance when the Houston Oilers of the newly created American Football League signed him as their quarterback. Although he was already 33 years old, Blanda threw 165 touchdown passes during his seven seasons in Houston. Blanda spent his final nine seasons with the Oakland Raiders, where his last-minute heroics as a quarterback and field-goal kicker made him a hero. By the time he finally retired at age 48 in 1975, George Blanda held records for the most seasons played (26), most games (340), and most points scored (2,002). Not bad for a 12th-round draft pick.

4. ROOSEVELT BROWN

Offensive tackle Roosevelt Brown was not chosen until the 27th round of the 1953 draft by the New York Giants. Brown had attended Morgan State, and players were rarely drafted from black colleges in those days. The only reason he was selected was because one of the Giants' executives had seen his photo in a black newspaper, *The Pittsburgh Courier.* It proved to be a shrewd pick as Roosevelt Brown went on to be a nine-time Pro Bowler and was inducted into the Pro Football Hall of Fame in 1975.

5. RAYMOND BERRY

It wasn't until the 20th round of the 1954 draft that the Baltimore Colts selected end Raymond Berry. At the time he seemed like a long shot to make the team. One of his legs was shorter than the other, he was nearsighted, and his back was so bad that he had to wear a corset. In college at Southern Methodist, he had caught only 33 passes and scored one touchdown. What Raymond Berry did have was determination. He would work on his pass patterns long after the regular practice sessions ended. At home he had his wife throw to him. His hard work paid off as Berry went on to become a five-time Pro Bowler, caught 631 passes, and scored 68 touchdowns during his 13 seasons in Baltimore.

6. ANDY ROBUSTELLI

Andy Robustelli, a defensive end from tiny Arnold College, was overlooked until the 19th round of the 1951 draft. Robustelli played five years with the Los Angeles Rams before joining the New York Giants in 1956. He enjoyed his greatest years in New York and was named to seven All-NFL teams during his Hall of Fame career.

7. DEACON JONES

Another defensive end from a small college (Mississippi Valley State), Deacon Jones was picked in the 14th round of the 1961 draft by the Los Angeles Rams. The man who coined the term "sack" was so difficult to block that he was usually double- or triple-teamed. The leader of the "Fearsome Foursome" defensive line—which included Merlin Olsen, Roosevelt Grier, and Lamar Lundy—Jones played in eight Pro Bowls and was the league's defensive player of the year in 1967 and 1968.

8. WILLIE DAVIS

Like Andy Robustelli and Deacon Jones, Willie Davis was a defensive end who was not originally considered NFL material.

Selected in the 15th round of the 1956 draft by Cleveland, Davis didn't emerge as a star until moving to Green Bay in 1960. Under Vince Lombardi's tutelage, Davis became the foundation of the Packer defense. Before he retired in 1969, Davis had played in five Pro Bowls and for five NFL championship teams.

9. DAN ABRAMOWICZ

Selected in the 17th round of the 1967 draft by the New Orleans Saints, wide receiver Dan Abramowicz was nearly cut in training camp. When called in to see coach Tom Fears, Abramowicz said, "You're not cutting me. You didn't give me a fair chance, and I'm not leaving." The flabbergasted coach decided to give him a second chance. Abramowicz rewarded him by catching 12 passes in his first game. During his eight-year career, he caught 369 passes for 5,686 yards and 39 touchdowns. At one point, he set an NFL record by making receptions in 105 consecutive games.

10. LEROY KELLY

Running back Leroy Kelly didn't get picked until the eighth round of the 1964 draft. Within a few years, the Cleveland Browns realized they had a worthy replacement for Jim Brown. Kelly led the NFL in rushing in 1967 and 1968 and scored 90 touchdowns during his Hall of Fame career.

THE UNDRAFTED

At least the players in the previous list were drafted. The following players did not hear their names called on draft day. Despite being undrafted, they all went on to NFL glory.

1. KURT WARNER

Kurt Warner is one of the great Cinderella stories in football history. For most of his college career he rode the bench at Northern Iowa. Undrafted, he was invited to the Green Bay Packers' training camp only to find himself behind two very talented quarterbacks, Brett Favre and Mark Brunell. Warner played three years with the Iowa Barnstormers of the Arena Football League. In 1997, he was promised a tryout with the Chicago Bears. Incredibly, he missed the tryout because he was bitten on the elbow by a spider during his honeymoon in Jamaica and was unable to throw. Warner finally got his opportunity in 1999 when St. Louis Rams' quarterback Trent Green was injured during a preseason game. Although he had completed only four passes prior to 1999, Warner threw

41 touchdown passes, becoming only the second quarterback in NFL history to throw more than 40 in a season. Kurt Warner was voted the NFL's Most Valuable Player and topped off his magical season with a victory in Super Bowl XXXIV.

2. NIGHT TRAIN LANE

After not being drafted, Dick Lane, a defensive back who played his college ball at Western Nebraska Community College, asked for a tryout with the Los Angeles Rams in 1952. Not only did Lane make the team, he set an interceptions record that still stands—Night Train picked off 14 passes in his rookie season and 68 in his 14-year career.

3. EMLEN TUNNELL

Undrafted, Emlen Tunnell, a defensive back from the University of Iowa, requested a tryout with the New York Giants in 1948. Tunnell starred with the Giants for 11 seasons and his 79 career interceptions rank second in NFL history. In 1967, he became the first African-American to be inducted into the Pro Football Hall of Fame.

4. WILLIE BROWN

Cornerback Willie Brown went undrafted and was cut during his first tryout with the Houston Oilers. Signed by the Denver Broncos in 1963, he tied an NFL record on November 15, 1964, when he intercepted four passes in a game against the New York Jets. Brown picked off 54 passes during his career with Denver and Oakland between 1963 and 1978. The master of the bump-and-run, Brown was inducted into the Pro Football Hall of Fame in 1984.

5. WILLIE WOOD

Willie Wood signed with the Green Bay Packers in 1960 after not being drafted. The defensive back was a cornerstone in the great Packer defense of the 1960s and led the league in interceptions with nine in 1962. He was elected to the Pro Football Hall of Fame in 1989.

6. JIM LANGER

An offensive lineman from South Dakota State, Jim Langer was not drafted. Invited to camp by the Dolphins in 1970, Langer spent ten seasons in Miami. One of the greatest centers in NFL history, he was inducted into the Pro Football Hall of Fame in 1987.

7. BILL PASCHAL

It didn't take undrafted Georgia Tech fullback Bill Paschal long to prove his detractors wrong. Paschal, playing for the New York Giants, led the NFL in rushing in 1943 and 1944, his first two seasons.

8. EVERSON WALLS

Everson Walls was another undrafted defensive back who achieved instant stardom. In 1981, the rookie cornerback for the Dallas Cowboys led the NFL in interceptions with 11. Walls intercepted 57 passes during his 13-year career.

9. JOE JACOBY

Despite not being drafted, offensive lineman Joe Jacoby played 13 seasons for the Washington Redskins. The six-foot, seven-inch, 305-pound Jacoby was the leader of the famed Redskins line known as the "Hogs." Jacoby played in four Pro Bowls and four Super Bowls.

10. JOHN SETTLE

Undrafted running back John Settle rushed for 1,024 yards for the Atlanta Falcons in 1988 and was selected to the Pro Bowl.

FOOTBALL'S JACKIE ROBINSONS

Unlike major-league baseball, professional football did not initially ban black athletes. From 1920 to 1933, 14 African-Americans played in the National Football League. However, no black players were permitted in the league from 1933 until 1946. The following ten athletes paved the way for future black stars.

1. WILLIAM HENRY LEWIS

The first African-American to play in a college football game was William Henry Lewis. He played his first game for Amherst in 1889, and by 1891, he was the team captain. The following year, Lewis became the first black player to be named to the All-American team. In 1911, he achieved another milestone when he became the first African-American to be admitted to the American Bar Association.

2. CHARLES FOLLIS

Charles Follis became the first black professional football player when he signed a contract to play for the Shelby (Ohio) Blues on September 15, 1904. The halfback, known as the "Black Cyclone," led his team to a 9–1 record. In a 1905 game against Toledo, Jack Tattersoll, the opposing captain, chafed at the racial slurs endured by Follis. "Don't call Follis a nigger," Tattersoll said. "He is a gentleman and a clean player."

3. **RUBE MARSHALL**

The first African-American to play in the American Football Association was end Roland "Rube" Marshall. On October 3, 1920, Marshall played for the Rock Island Independents in a game against the Muncie Flyers.

4. **FRITZ POLLARD**

Halfback Fritz Pollard scored 12 touchdowns during his professional career, which lasted from 1920 to 1926. In 1921, he became the first black head coach in the NFL. Sharing coaching duties with Elgie Tobin, Pollard's Akron Pros finished the season with a record of 8–3–1.

5. **KENNY WASHINGTON**

Kenny Washington can lay claim to being the Jackie Robinson of professional football. In 1939, the UCLA tailback led the nation in total yards from scrimmage with 1,370. Unable to play in the NFL, Washington spent five years with the Hollywood Bears, earning $50 to $100 a game. On March 21, 1946, Washington broke the color barrier in the NFL by signing with the Los Angeles Rams. Some players intentionally tried to injure Washington by kneeing him and piling on. "It's hell to be a Negro," he told a teammate. Kenny Washington averaged more than six yards per carry during his three-year pro career. Overshadowed by Jackie Robinson, Washington began playing pro football a year before Robinson broke the color barrier in major league baseball.

6. WOODY STRODE

End Woody Strode caught four passes for the Los Angeles Rams in 1946 as a 32-year-old rookie. After his football career was over, Strode became a successful film actor.

7. GEORGE TALIAFERRO

George Taliaferro was the first African-American to be drafted by an NFL team. In 1949, the Indiana University halfback was selected by the Chicago Bears in the 13th round. Taliaferro scored 21 touchdowns during his six-year NFL career.

8. WILLIE THROWER

The man with a perfect name for a quarterback, Willie Thrower played in only one NFL game, but it was a milestone. On October 18, 1953, Thrower, playing for the Chicago Bears against the San Francisco Forty-Niners, became the first black NFL quarterback. He completed three of eight passes for 27 yards.

9. ART SHELL

Offensive tackle Art Shell was an eight-time Pro Bowler with the Oakland Raiders. In 1989, Shell became the first black coach of the modern era when he led the Raiders to a 7–5 record. A head coach for six seasons, Shell's record was an outstanding 54 wins and 38 losses.

10. MARION MOTLEY

Professional football's first superstar was Cleveland fullback Marion Motley. He averaged more than eight yards a carry in his rookie season and led the NFL in rushing in 1950. Motley was inducted into the Pro Football Hall of Fame in 1968.

OUTRAGEOUS OWNERS

The NFL has come a long way since its inception in 1920. In those days, an investor could buy a franchise for $100. In today's market, a team like the Washington Redskins can cost as much as $800 million. With this kind of money at stake, naturally some owners are inclined to take a hands-on approach to their investments. Here are some owners who put their mouths where their money is.

1. WALTER LINGO

Although Walter Lingo had absolutely no interest in football, he paid $100 for a professional franchise in 1922. His team, the Oorang Indians, was named after his dog kennel located in LaRue, Ohio. Lingo had the novel idea of fielding a team comprised of Native American players. In their two-year existence, the Oorang Indians played only one home game. The whole purpose of the team was to promote Lingo's prized Airedales in other cities. Even though his team included the great Jim Thorpe, the game was secondary to the halftime show. Lingo had his players do Indian dances and toss tomahawks to entertain the crowd. One unfortunate player, Nikolas Lassa, was forced to wrestle a bear. The Indian acts were mere preliminaries to the show-stopping finale. Lingo directed his players to reenact a World War I battle between American and German troops. As the battle raged, "Red Cross," a trained Airedale from the Oorang Kennel, administered first aid to the wounded soldiers. One of Lingo's Airedales cost up to $150, more than he paid for his team franchise. The Oorang Indians folded after the 1923 season with a record of three wins and sixteen losses, making the team one of the NFL's biggest dogs.

2. **HARRY WISMER**

Harry Wismer's motto could have been "The buck stops here." The owner of the 1962 New York Titans of the American Football League, Wismer had difficulty meeting payrolls. His checks bounced more often than the team's incomplete passes. At one practice, the team bus didn't arrive because Wismer had failed to pay for the charter. The Titan players were forced to hitch rides back to their hotel. On paydays, players raced to the bank with their checks, hoping to cash them before Wismer's account ran dry. One of the reasons for Wismer's financial difficulties was poor attendance. For the 1962 season, only 36,400 fans paid to see the Titans play. New York finished the season in last place in the Eastern Division.

3. **BUD HUCUL**

If anyone could give Harry Wismer a run for his money as the poorest owner, it would have to be Bud Hucul, owner of the Detroit Wheels of the ill-fated World Football League. On one occasion, his team couldn't get their uniforms from the laundry because Hucul had failed to pay the bill. By the time the season ended, Hucul was in debt to more than 120 creditors. The Wheels finished the 1974 season with the league's worst record, one win and 13 losses.

4. FRAN MANACO

The Jacksonville Sharks, owned by Fran Manaco, finished last in the Eastern Division of the World Football League in 1974. Swimming in a sea of red ink, Manaco was forced to borrow $27,000 from head coach Bud Asher to meet payroll. The owner later showed his appreciation by firing Asher.

5. ROBERT IRSAY

Robert Irsay will forever be remembered as the man who moved the Colts out of Baltimore. In 1972, Irsay, the owner of the Los Angeles Rams, traded his team to Carroll Rosenbloom in exchange for the Baltimore Colts. Under his control, one of football's most storied franchises was quickly turned into an also-ran. The Colts selected quarterback John Elway with the first pick of the 1983 NFL draft, but were forced to trade him to the Denver Broncos when Elway refused to sign. On March 29, 1987, in the middle of the night, a convoy of moving vans left the Colts' headquarters, headed for Indianapolis. Irsay had sneaked out of town.

6. ART MODELL

When Baltimore finally got a new team in 1996, it was at the expense of Cleveland. Art Modell bought the Cleveland Browns in 1961. The next season he fired Paul Brown, who had coached the team to seven championships and whose record in Cleveland was 158 wins, 48 losses, and eight ties. Despite having attendance that averaged more than 70,000 per game in Cleveland, Modell moved the team to Baltimore to take advantage of a lucrative deal which included a publicly funded stadium.

7. GEORGE PRESTON MARSHALL

George Preston Marshall is a member of the Pro Football Hall of Fame. His innovations included divisional play and an increased passing game. One of football's greatest showmen, Marshall suggested that football had derived from Roman gladiator contests. In 1937, he moved his Boston Redskins to Washington. During the early days of the franchise, Marshall ordered his players to entertain the fans at halftime by putting on face paint and performing a war dance. When his star player, Cliff Battles, asked for a $500 raise after leading the league in rushing, Marshall refused. Battles was so incensed that he retired from football rather than play for Marshall. In 1945, the owner drafted UCLA's Cal Rossi even though he still had a year of college eligibility. The next year, Marshall again used a first-round pick to select Rossi, who informed the Redskins that he had no interest in playing for them. One of Marshall's most shameful stances was his refusal to sign African-American players. He told quarterback Sammy Baugh that he'd start signing black players when the Harlem Globetrotters began using white players. The Redskins were the last NFL team to integrate. Bobby Mitchell, a star wide receiver, joined the team in 1962.

8. BERT BELL

Bert Bell bought the Philadelphia Eagles for $4,500 in 1936. He coached his team from 1936 to 1940, compiling a dismal record of ten wins, 44 losses, and two ties. Bell helped conceive the inaugural NFL draft in 1936. That first year Bell drafted nine players, including first pick Jay Berwanger, but was unable to sign any of them. Bell co-owned the Pittsburgh Steelers from 1941 to 1946. During his tenure, the Steelers finished last three times, including a winless season in 1944.

9. MIKE BROWN

Mike Brown is living proof that football acumen is not hereditary. The son of the legendary Paul Brown, Mike assumed control of the Cincinnati Bengals after his father's death in 1991. In 1992, Brown hired Dave Shula, son of Don Shula, as the Bengals' head coach. After all, Dave's father was the winningest coach in NFL history. It seemed logical that his son might have inherited some of his coaching skill. By the time he was fired in 1996, Dave Shula had compiled a record of 19 wins and 52 losses. The Bengals, a team which had played in the 1989 Super Bowl, set an NFL record in the 1990s for the most losses in a decade.

10. ART MCBRIDE

The original owner of the Cleveland Browns, Art McBride also owned a taxi cab company. He gave his reserve players jobs as cab drivers. This was the origin of the term "taxi squad."

CRAZY LEGS AND TIPPY TOES

Sometimes a football player's nickname is more well known than his given name. Most fans knew Boomer Esiason by his nickname rather than by his first name, Norman. Everyone's heard of Notre Dame's Four Horsemen backfield, but how many people could actually name them? (Elmer Layden, Jim Crowley, Don Miller, and Harry Stuhldreher.) How many people could tell you that running back Cookie Gilchrist's real name was Carlton? Here are some of football's most colorful nicknames.

1. THE HUMAN BOWLING BALL

At first glance, Don Nottingham didn't look much like a football player. Short and round, he resembled a bowling ball. Of the 442 players selected in the 1971 draft, Nottingham was the 441st pick. During his seven years in the NFL with Baltimore and Miami, Nottingham rolled through the opposition for nearly 2,500 yards and 35 touchdowns.

2. CRAZY LEGS

End Elroy Hirsch was known as "Crazy Legs" because of his zig-zag running style. He was so elusive that he averaged more than 18 yards a catch during his career with the Los Angeles Rams, which lasted from 1949 to 1957. His greatest season was 1951, when he caught 66 passes for 1,495 yards and 17 touchdowns. Hirsch announced his retirement at the end of the 1954 season. On December 12, 1954, fans in Los Angeles paid tribute to him at halftime of a game against Green Bay. During the ceremony, hundreds of fans came out of the stands and began tearing the uniform off their hero. They carried off his jersey, shoulder pads, and anything else they could grab. Hirsch removed his pants and shoes and tossed them into the adoring crowd. By the time the souvenir frenzy was over, the only thing Hirsch was wearing were his hip pads and shorts. Crazy Legs changed his mind about quitting and played three more years.

3. THE REFRIGERATOR

Defensive tackle William Perry was nicknamed "The Refrigerator" because of his frequent trips to the icebox. The 335-pounder was as large as a refrigerator. Occasionally, Bears' coach Mike Ditka used Perry as a blocking back or fullback. On November 17, 1985, the Refrigerator picked up halfback Walter Payton and tried to carry him over the goal line. The officials whistled Perry for illegal use of the hands and penalized the Bears ten yards. Perry's greatest moment came when he rushed for a touchdown in Chicago's 46–10 victory over the New England Patriots in Super Bowl XX. When asked to name his biggest weakness, the Refrigerator replied, "Cheeseburgers."

4. HACKSAW

Jack Reynolds played linebacker for the Los Angeles Rams and San Francisco Forty-Niners from 1970 to 1984. The two-time

Pro Bowler was given his nickname, "Hacksaw," because of an incident in college. After his Tennessee Volunteers lost a game 38–0 to Mississippi in 1969, Reynolds decided to take out his anger on a 1953 Chevy. He decided to saw the car in half. It took Reynolds two days and 14 hacksaw blades to finish the job.

5. **BAMBI**

Wide receiver Lance Alworth was nicknamed "Bambi" because he ran like a deer and leaped like a gazelle. Alworth played for San Diego and Dallas between 1962 and 1972. Bambi caught 542 passes for more than 10,000 yards and scored 87 touchdowns.

6. **THE MAD BOMBER**

Quarterback Daryle Lamonica was known as the "Mad Bomber" because of his long touchdown passes. His greatest seasons came with the Oakland Raiders. Lamonica's favorite targets were receivers Warren Wells and Fred Biletnikoff. Lamonica was the American Football League's Most Valuable Player in 1967 and 1969.

7. **THE GALLOPING GHOST**

Harold "Red" Grange was one of the best running backs in college football history. On October 18, 1924, Grange played his greatest game for Illinois, gaining 402 yards and scoring five touchdowns in a 39–14 rout of Michigan. Sportswriter Grantland Rice nicknamed Grange "The Galloping Ghost" because of his phantom-like ability to elude tacklers. The nickname was much catchier than his previous monicker, the "Wheaton Iceman."

8. BEAR

Paul Bryant coached the Alabama Crimson Tide to six national championships. He retired in 1982 with 323 wins. Bryant got his nickname for wrestling a bear at a carnival when he was 14 years old.

9. TIPPY TOES AND MAD DUCK

For 12 seasons, Alex Karras was a top-notch defensive tackle for the Detroit Lions. Karras was nicknamed "Tippy Toes" because of his agility and "Mad Duck" for his belligerent nature.

10. BAD GIRL

Red Badgro played end for New York and Brooklyn from 1927 to 1936. The Hall of Famer's nickname, "Bad Girl," was a variation on his last name.

THE NAME GAME

Some people are born to be football players. Philadelphia Eagles' wide receiver Mike Quick had the perfect name for his position. Dallas Cowboys' defensive back Eric Hurt had a name which described the violent nature of his sport. How's this for a roster of football names?

1. MARION RUSHING

The possessor of the ultimate football name, Marion Rushing played linebacker for Chicago, St. Louis, Atlanta, and Houston between 1959 and 1968. The only thing that would have been better was if Rushing had been a running back. Another player, Tyrone Rush, did play running back for the 1994 Washington Redskins.

2. JIM KIICK

Jim Kiick didn't punt or kick the ball, but he gained more than 6,000 yards during his career as a rusher and receiver. Kiick is best known as a member of the Miami Dolphins Super Bowl champions of the early 1970s.

3. JACK SACK

Jack Sack was a lineman with Columbus in 1923 and Canton in 1926.

4. CLARK GAINES

Clark Gaines lived up to his name by gaining more than 2,500 yards as a running back for the New York Jets and Kansas City Chiefs from 1976 to 1982.

5. WILLIE THROWER

Willie Thrower was ideally named for a quarterback. The Michigan State signal caller played one game for the Chicago Bears in 1953.

6. JACK SPIKES

What better name for a place kicker than Jack Spikes? He played for the Dallas Texans, Kansas City Chiefs, Houston Oilers, and Buffalo Bills from 1960 to 1967.

7. GARY DOWNS

Running back Gary Downs made his NFL debut with the New York Giants in 1994 and has since played for the Denver Broncos and Atlanta Falcons.

8. SAM HOLDEN

Sam Holden was an offensive tackle who played college football at Grambling. Perhaps because he lived up to his name, Holden played in only nine games for the 1971 New Orleans Saints.

9. **MAC SPEEDIE**

End Mac Speedie used his speed to catch 349 passes and score 34 touchdowns for the Cleveland Browns from 1946 to 1952.

10. **TOM WHAM**

Defensive end Tom Wham played for the Chicago Cardinals from 1949 to 1951. His name reminds us that football is a collision sport.

MAD STORKS

Football is also a team sport, but these players never had any trouble maintaining their individuality.

1. TIM ROSSOVICH

Football's ultimate flake, Tim Rossovich, played linebacker and defensive end for the Philadelphia Eagles, San Diego Chargers, and Houston Oilers from 1968 to 1976. If you are what you eat, Tim Rossovich was something else. He ate spiders, lit cigarettes, even a beer mug. Rossovich once challenged Mike Ditka to a bottle opening contest in which they used only their teeth. It was no contest—Rossovich won by the score of 100 to three. You never knew what would happen when Rossovich opened his mouth. On one occasion a baby sparrow flew out. He never had any trouble being noticed. He liked to dress in a Dracula cape or wizard outfit. He ran through the streets wearing only shaving cream. Rossovich sunbathed with "Unidentified Flying Object" written on his chest. He preferred to sleep face down on hotel room floors with a compass near his head. He always made certain that his head pointed due north so that the earth's magnetic waves would revitalize him. When not sleeping in his room,

Rossovich might be found standing on his head in the hotel lobby with his face immersed in a bucket of ice water.

2. JOHNNY BLOOD

A Hall of Fame halfback who played in the NFL from 1925 to 1938, Johnny Blood starred on four Green Bay Packers' championship teams. If there were a Hall of Fame for flakes, he would be a charter member. Johnny McNally chose the name Blood after seeing the Rudolph Valentino film, *Blood and Sand.* He so identified with the name that he once slashed his arm so that he could sign an autograph in blood. His play on the field could be infuriating. He sometimes dropped easy passes and turned routine plays into spectacular catches. The speedy receiver once waited on the five-yard line for defenders to catch up to him, then dragged them across the goal line for a touchdown. Many of Blood's shenanigans had to do with trains. He was called the "Hobo Halfback" because he rode the rails to Green Bay in 1932. On another occasion he ran across the top of a moving train. After missing the team train in Wisconsin, Blood raced in his automobile to catch up. A half hour later, he sat on the fender of his car, which was blocking the train tracks. The locomotive came to a stop only a few feet from the car and Blood calmly boarded the train.

3. JOE DON LOONEY

If ever a player had a name that described his behavior, it was Joe Don Looney. The fullback, known as "Football's Magnificent Misfit," played for Baltimore, Detroit, Washington, and New Orleans from 1964 to 1969. A coach's nightmare, he opposed authority in any form. He refused to practice because he said he already knew all the plays. He intentionally ignored his blockers because, in his own words, "Anyone can run where the holes are." During one of his infrequent practices, Looney savagely attacked the tackling dummy.

4. TED HENDRICKS

At six feet seven inches tall and weighing two hundred and twenty pounds, Ted Hendricks was nicknamed "The Mad Stork." The Hall of Fame linebacker intercepted 26 passes for the Baltimore Colts and Oakland Raiders between 1969 and 1983. At the Raiders training camp, Hendricks mounted a white horse that was grazing in an adjoining field. Hendricks galloped onto the playing field, dismounted, and began practice as if nothing out of the ordinary had occurred.

5. JOHN RIGGINS

Inducted into the Pro Football Hall of Fame in 1992, running back John Riggins rushed for 11,352 and scored 116 touchdowns while playing for the Washington Redskins and New York Jets. His greatest season was 1983 when he scored 24 touchdowns and rushed for 1,347 yards. As a rookie with the Jets in 1971, Riggins made an impression on the first day of practice. He arrived in camp riding a motorcycle. Riggins wore an oversized derby with a big red feather on it, no shirt, baggy pants, and storm-trooper boots. His favorite haircut was a mohawk. At a black-tie fundraiser in 1985, Riggins fell asleep on the floor during a speech delivered by Vice President George Bush. Washington teammate Russ Grimm described Riggins best when he remarked, "Some guys march to the beat of a different drummer. John had his own band."

6. HOLLYWOOD HENDERSON

Thomas "Hollywood" Henderson played linebacker for the Dallas Cowboys from 1975 to 1979. Henderson claimed that he was the greatest linebacker who ever lived. At practice, he once stepped out of a limousine wearing a full-length mink coat. Another time, in a game in which the Cowboys were leading Los Angeles 28–0, Hollywood picked up the pom-pom of a Rams' cheerleader and began mocking the opposition. Henderson hit the jackpot in 2000 when he won $28 million in the Texas lottery.

7. MIKE PRICE

Washington State coach Mike Price is a master of disguise. Before a game against the Oregon Ducks, he dressed in a hunting outfit and carried a shotgun. Oregon players were sitting ducks for Price and his Cougars, losing 51–38. Prior to a 1989 game against the Arizona State Sun Devils, Price dressed in a devil's costume, complete with red tights, horns, cape, and pitchfork. This time the strategy backfired as the Sun Devils prevailed 44–39.

8. BRIAN BOSWORTH

Oklahoma's Brian Bosworth won the Butkus Award as college football's best linebacker in 1985 and 1986. Hampered by injuries, Bosworth played only three years with the Seattle Seahawks. Bosworth was such a great self promoter that you would have thought he was the second coming of Dick Butkus. Boz parlayed his notoriety into a brief career as an action film star, appearing in such movies as *One Tough Bastard* and *Midnight Heat.*

9. JIM MCMAHON

Best remembered for leading the Chicago Bears to victory in Super Bowl XX, quarterback Jim McMahon was one of football's free spirits. During Super Bowl week, McMahon dropped his pants and mooned a helicopter flying overhead. He was fined by the NFL for wearing headbands with messages written on them. At one public appearance, McMahon guzzled a twelve-pack of beer.

10. OTIS SISTRUNK

A two-time All-Pro defensive lineman with the Oakland Raiders, Otis Sistrunk was one of football's great eccentrics. Sistrunk did not attend college, prompting Alex Karras to comment that he attended the University of Mars.

PRACTICAL JOKERS

If there were an All-Pro team for practical jokers, these players would be named to the first team.

1. LARRY CSONKA

Running back Larry Csonka was a 1,000-yard rusher for the Miami Dolphins from 1971 to 1973. He rushed for more than 100 yards in Miami's victories in Super Bowls VII and VIII. Csonka and defensive end Manny Fernandez played a memorable practical joke on coach Don Shula. Csonka and Fernandez placed a baby alligator in Shula's shower at the Dolphins training headquarters. They laughed hysterically as their normally calm coach ran naked out of the shower.

2. MIKE BARBER

Another alligator prank was pulled by Mike Barber, an All-Pro tight end with the Houston Oilers in the late 1970s. He found a dead alligator on a roadside in Louisiana. Barber brought it back to the Oilers' training camp and put it in a room where the team's defensive backs met to watch game films. He waited outside until he heard the players scream.

At that point, Barber rushed into the room and saved them from their imminent peril.

3. **CHARLIE KRUEGER**

Charlie Krueger was a dependable defensive lineman who played for the San Francisco Forty-Niners from 1959 to 1973. At the Forty-Niners training camp, he found a small tree frog and decided to put it in guard Howard Mudd's chewing tobacco. Mudd realized something was wrong when he placed the wad in his mouth. Rather than acknowledge the joke, Mudd endured the entire practice session without spitting out the frog.

4. **LYLE BLACKWOOD**

Rookies are often the butt of practical jokes. Lyle Blackwood, a defensive back for the Bengals, Seahawks, Colts, and Dolphins from 1973 to 1986, loved to pull the "wronged husband" routine on unsuspecting rookies. During a game, he would point out a beautiful woman in the stands. He would tell the gullible player that the woman had a crush on him and wanted to arrange a rendezvous. The only problem was that the woman was married. Blackwood offered to act as a go-between. When the unsuspecting Romeo arrived for his meeting with the mystery woman, her "husband" jumped out from behind the bushes with a shotgun and fired blanks. Victims of the joke ran for their lives. One terrified player ran for five hours before being found.

5. **DAN DIERDORF**

Dan Dierdorf, the Hall of Fame St. Louis Cardinals' offensive lineman, played a classic practical joke on teammate Conrad Dobler in 1975. Dobler, who prided himself on his reputation as football's dirtiest player, was preparing for a television interview at the Cardinals' training camp in St. Charles, Missouri. He was going to be interviewed by Phyllis George, a former Miss America, and he wanted to make a good impression. Dobler spent an hour getting ready so he'd look his best. Dierdorf spotted Dobler's new pair of slacks and cut off one of the legs with a pair of scissors. When Dobler put on the pants, he realized what had happened and, in a rage, began tearing up the locker room. Tight end Jackie Smith offered Dobler a pair of pants, which were a size too small. Dobler had little choice but to wear them during the interview.

6. GREGG BINGHAM

Houston linebacker Gregg Bingham didn't care too much for his teammate Thomas "Hollywood" Henderson, who had come to the Oilers from Dallas in 1980. During a flight, Henderson excused himself to go to the bathroom. Bingham realized that by applying pressure to an adjoining door, he could cause the restroom door to jam. As a result, Hollywood Henderson spent more than an hour trapped in the restroom.

7. TIM ROSSOVICH

The life of every party, a nude Tim Rossovich once did a back flip into a wedding cake. At another party, the unsuspecting host opened the door to find Rossovich on fire. He walked into the room, turned around, and left. Rossovich had doused himself with lighter fluid and knew that he had forty seconds before he would be burned.

8. JOE MONTANA

Quarterback Joe Montana was a three-time NFL Most Valuable Player and led the San Francisco Forty-Niners to four Super Bowl victories. Teammates discovered that he was a tireless practical joker. The Forty-Niners' training camp was located at Sierra College in Rocklin, California. Many players used bicycles to get to the remote training site. Montana delighted in letting the air out of the tires and locking the bikes together with a chain. His most elaborate prank was to hide the bicycles in trees.

9. TIM WILSON

Tim Wilson, a fullback with the Houston Oilers from 1977 to 1982, was responsible for another training camp practical joke. He rigged the elevator so that fireworks would go off when someone opened the door. Star running back Earl Campbell was one of the unfortunate Oilers present when the fireworks started. Players ran for their lives, and one jumped into the broom closet.

10. WALTER PAYTON

The NFL's all-time leading rusher, Walter Payton liked to have fun at the expense of his Chicago Bears teammates. Once, during a morning training camp meeting, he frightened everyone by setting off fireworks. A Payton specialty was goosing his teammates while they were being interviewed on television.

MEMORABLE MASCOTS

Many college and professional teams have mascots. These team symbols can be either a person dressed in a costume or an animal. These memorable mascots were worth watching.

1. SEBASTIAN THE IBIS

Sebastian the Ibis can best be described as looking like a disgruntled duck. The University of Miami mascot was in rare form during a game against the Florida State Seminoles on September 28, 1989. The Seminoles mascot, Chief Osceola, rode around the field on horseback, carrying a flaming lance. Sebastian, wearing a fireman's hat, tried to put out the flame with a fire extinguisher. The amateur firefighter was handcuffed by security guards and led off the field.

2. AUBURN WAR EAGLE

Florida Gators' wide receiver Wes Chandler incurred the wrath of the Auburn War Eagle during the final moments of a game played on October 30, 1976. With time running out and Florida trailing 19–17, Chandler caught a pass and ran 80 yards for the winning score. Just as he was about to cross the goal line, he was attacked by the Auburn War Eagle, which had escaped from its handler. The bird pecked Chandler mercilessly, and Auburn was penalized 15 yards on the ensuing kickoff for unsportsmanlike conduct.

3. BEVO

The Texas Longhorns' mascot, Bevo, has a long and tarnished history since being introduced in 1916. The first Bevo was served at a Longhorns' dinner banquet, and his successors seem to have been trying to get revenge ever since. The second Bevo charged an SMU cheerleader, who managed to fend him off with a megaphone. Bevo III escaped from his pen and terrorized the Texas campus. Bevo IV attacked a parked car. The next Bevo broke loose and scattered the Baylor band.

4. THOR

For their first game in Atlanta Stadium in 1966, the Falcons planned a surprise for their fans. A falcon named Thor had been trained to fly three times around the stadium and return. Officials proudly released Thor, but, instead of circling the field, the bird flew out of sight. Three more times falcons were released, all with the same result.

5. BILLY GOAT

The rivalry between Army and Navy is one of the longest and most intense in college football. That rivalry carried over to the mascots. During the pregame ceremony for the 1946 game, a huge replica of the Army mule was wheeled out. As the cadets stood up to cheer, a trap door opened and out came the Navy mascot, Billy Goat, with the Navy cheerleaders. The Trojan mule was just one of many incidents involving the mascots. In 1953, Army cadets kidnapped Billy Goat, but the joke proved to be on them. The cantankerous goat ate the upholstery of the getaway car, kicked out the rear window, and punched a hole in the roof.

6. GUMBO

One of the most reluctant mascots was Gumbo, the New Orleans Saints' Saint Bernard. The first Gumbo, perhaps disheartened by the Saints' poor play, ran away. Gumbo II drank beer before the game and usually sat by the fence and whined to be let out. Once he chased a Pittsburgh Steelers' quarterback across the goal line for a touchdown. His successor had to be dragged to work. After urinating on the field, he would curl up and go to sleep. In the same tradition, Gumbo IV pooped on the field almost every game.

7. SEAL

Another dog with a small bladder, Seal, the mascot for the University of Virginia from 1947 to 1953, made a tradition of urinating on opposing cheerleaders' megaphones. His favorite target for a leg-up was the goalposts.

8. REVEILLE

On November 17, 1973, the Rice band paid tribute to Reveille, the Texas A&M collie mascot, during their halftime show. The band formed a giant puddle next to a fire hydrant. Aggie fans were not amused, and the band required police protection. Rice won the game 24–20.

9. SOONER SCHOONER

The Sooner Schooner was a tiny covered wagon pulled by two white ponies. Anytime Oklahoma scored, the wagon circled the field in celebration. In the fourth quarter of the 1985 Orange Bowl, Oklahoma and Washington were tied 14–14 when Tim Lasher apparently kicked a go-ahead 22-yard field goal. The Sooner Schooner roared onto the field, prematurely it turned out. The field goal was negated by a five-yard illegal procedure penalty. To make matters worse, the officials tacked on another 15-yard penalty for unsportsmanlike conduct because the wagon had come out onto the field. Lasher missed the 42-yard field goal attempt, and Oklahoma went on to lose the game, 28–17.

10. **BOWS-O**

One of the most short-lived mascots was Bows-O. In 1989, the University of Hawaii decided they needed a mascot. The result was Bows-O, a gap-toothed mascot who made his debut at the annual homecoming game. The fans immediately began to shower the puffy-headed figure with garbage and insults. Before the next game, Bows-O was history.

UNIFORM BEHAVIOR

Football teams have been wearing uniforms since 1874. In that year, Harvard played McGill. The Harvard players wore sweaters and tied handkerchiefs around their heads. The McGill uniforms consisted of striped jerseys, white pants, and turbans. Over the years there have been some unconventional uniforms. The Duluth Eskimos, who were part of the National Football League from 1923 to 1927, had igloos on their jerseys. The 1934 St. Louis Gunners featured a cannon on their uniforms.

1. ELMER LAYDEN

In 1945, National Football League Commissioner Elmer Layden ruled that all players must wear long stockings. The reason behind the ruling was that Layden believed most players had ugly legs.

2. THE 1962 DENVER BRONCOS

The 1962 Denver Broncos' uniforms may have been the most hideous on record. The brown and gold uniforms were drab, but it was the brown and white vertical striped socks that made them reviled. The team wisely changed its uniform colors to orange and blue. The hated uniforms were taken out and burned.

3. EDGAR ALLAN POE

Edgar Allan Poe was an All-American back at Princeton. The grand nephew of the famed author, Poe invented a nose protector, the first face-guard, in 1890. The leather proboscis hung from a strap tied around the forehead. The bottom part of the device was held in place by clinched teeth. The device was so devious that it could have been an instrument of torture imagined by the original Poe in one of his horror stories. The primitive nose protector obstructed both the vision and breathing of the wearer and was soon abandoned.

4. GEORGE RATTERMAN

Cleveland Browns' coach Paul Brown wanted a new way to send signals to his quarterback, George Ratterman. In 1956, Brown devised a radio receiver which he installed in Ratterman's helmet. They decided to test the device in an isolated wooded area to avoid detection. Ratterman was arrested by the police as he wandered along a road trying to pick up the signals. When they tried it in a game, Ratterman somehow picked up a conversation between two women. To make matters worse, opposing coaches set up receivers to steal the signals. The experiment was abandoned, and helmet receivers were banned for many years.

5. POP WARNER

Glenn "Pop" Warner won 319 games during a college coaching career that spanned from 1895 to 1938. In 1905, at Cornell, he introduced numbers on uniforms. Seven years later, while coaching at Carlisle, he declared his opposition to helmets. According to Warner, players who did not wear helmets had more confidence, fewer head jolts, and kept their ears from being torn.

6. NORM EVANS

Tackle Norm Evans played for Houston, Miami, and Seattle from 1965 to 1978. This 250-pound lineman said that the hardest part of training camp was getting used to wearing the helmet. Evans had trouble holding his head up. The weight of the helmet caused his head to tilt to one side or the other. He had to do exercises to strengthen his neck.

7. STEVE OWEN

The New York Giants, coached by Steve Owen, were huge underdogs in the 1934 NFL Championship game against the Chicago Bears. The Bears were the defending NFL champions and entered the game undefeated. The title game was played on an icy field at the Polo Grounds. Chicago led 10–3 at half-time as players had trouble with their footing on the treacherous field. Giants' captain Ray Flaherty suggested that the team switch to sneakers. Owen sent equipment manager Abe Cohen to nearby Manhattan College to get the sneakers. With better traction, the Giants dominated the second half and upset the Bears 30–13.

8. FRANK NAUMETZ

Frank Naumetz, a linebacker for the Los Angeles Rams in the late 1940s, was such a hard hitter that he split nine plastic helmets in one season. NFL executives determined that the helmets offered more risk than protection and banned them for the 1948 season. They were reintroduced the following season.

9. FRED GEHRKE

One of Naumetz's Rams' teammates, halfback Fred Gehrke, had studied art at the University of Utah. In the late 1940s, he began painting rams' horns on the team's helmets. Unfortunately, the paint kept chipping off. By 1949, it was possible to bake the logos into the helmets, and helmet designs became widespread.

10. LYNDON JOHNSON

Lyndon Johnson liked to joke that political rival Gerald Ford had played without a helmet during his years at Michigan from 1932 to 1934. Johnson was correct; helmets weren't mandatory in college football until 1939.

GOOD THINGS COME IN SMALL PACKAGES

For the most part, football is played by huge men. Over the years, however, a few small men have succeeded in this large man's world.

1. DAVEY O'BRIEN

Only five feet, seven inches tall and 150 pounds, quarterback Davey O'Brien led Texas Christian to the national championship in 1938 and won the Heisman Trophy. As an NFL rookie in 1939 with the Philadelphia Eagles, he led the league in passing yardage. The next season he led NFL quarterbacks in completions. O'Brien retired after the 1940 season to join the FBI.

2. BUTCH MEEKER

One of the smallest players in NFL history, tailback Butch Meeker was five feet, three inches tall and weighed just over 140 pounds. "Shorty" Meeker scored two touchdowns during his rookie season with Providence.

3. BUDDY YOUNG

Despite being only five-foot four, halfback Buddy Young scored 13 touchdowns at Illinois in 1944, tying the school record set by the legendary Red Grange. Young was the Most Valuable Player of the 1947 College All-Star game. During his professional career, which lasted from 1947 to 1955, Young scored 44 touchdowns and accounted for nearly 10,000 total yards. One of the league's best return men, he ran back a kickoff 104 yards in a 1953 game against Philadelphia.

4. GUS DORAIS

At five feet, seven inches tall and 140 pounds, quarterback Gus Dorais seems an unlikely Notre Dame legend. Yet, it was Dorais who led the Fighting Irish to their first undefeated season in 1912. On November 1, 1913, Dorais quarterbacked Notre Dame to a 35–13 upset of unbeaten Army in the game that popularized the forward pass.

5. NOLAND SMITH

Few kickoff-return men generated excitement like Noland "Super Gnat" Smith. The five-foot five, 154-pound Smith played for Kansas City and San Francisco from 1967 to 1969. The highlight of his short career was a 106-yard kickoff return against Denver on December 17, 1967. Smith's nickname, Super Gnat, referred not only to his size, but also to his hobby of collecting insects.

6. JOEY STERNAMAN

Joey Sternaman could do it all as a player. During his eight seasons in professional football, he played quarterback on offense, safety on defense, and was a place kicker. In 1924, he led the league in scoring, and the following year he outscored and outgained his celebrated teammate, Red Grange. During his years in Chicago, a sportswriter once described Sternaman as a combination of "a bantam rooster and a pit bulldog." Sternaman achieved all this despite being only five feet, six inches tall and weighing only 150 pounds.

7. MACK HERRON

Five-foot, five-inch Mack Herron played running back for New England and Atlanta from 1973 to 1975. Herron led the NFL in kickoff return yards as a rookie and in 1974 scored 12 touchdowns.

8. ALBIE BOOTH

Known for his spectacular breakaway runs, Albie Booth starred for Yale from 1929 to 1931. The five-foot, six-inch, 155-pound halfback was nicknamed "The Mighty Atom" and "Little Boy Blue."

9. JACK DANIELS

Something of a mystery man, Jack Daniels was only 16 years old when he played one game for Milwaukee in 1925. The 135-pound tailback is one of the smallest players in NFL history.

10. ROLLIN ROACH

Rollin Roach scored a touchdown in his only game with the 1927 Chicago Cardinals. There is no record of why he was cut, but it probably had something to do with him being a 145-pound fullback.

HEAVYWEIGHTS

Players are much larger than they were when professional football began 80 years ago. In the 1920s, Gus Sonnenberg, who weighed less than 200 pounds, was an All-Pro lineman. Today, the average offensive lineman weighs more than 300 pounds. When William "The Refrigerator" Perry came into the league in 1984, the 335-pounder set a new standard for size. All of the following players outweighed The Refrigerator.

1. DAVID DIXON

David Dixon was born in New Zealand and played college football at Arizona State. The 354-pound guard joined the Minnesota Vikings in 1994 and became a starter the following season.

2. JOHN RAY

John Ray was a six-foot, eight-inch, 350-pound offensive tackle for the Indianapolis Colts in 1993.

3. LOUIS AGE

An 11th-round draft choice out of Southwestern Louisiana, 350-pound Louis Age played six games for the 1992 Chicago Bears.

4. JEROME DANIELS

Another 350-pounder, Jerome Daniels played eight games at offensive tackle for the 1998 Arizona Cardinals.

5. KOREY STRINGER

When tackle Korey Stringer was drafted by Minnesota in 1995, the 350-pound tackle was not even the heaviest lineman on the team. Guard David Dixon outweighed him by about five pounds.

6. JON KIRKSEY

Like David Dixon, Jon Kirksey was a 350-pound lineman who played at Arizona State. The defensive lineman played 11 games for the 1996 St. Louis Rams.

7. TRA THOMAS

Offensive tackle Tra Thomas played at Florida State. The six-foot, seven-inch, 350-pound Thomas was a first-round draft pick by the Philadelphia Eagles in 1998.

8. JERRY CRAFTS

Jerry Crafts, a 344-pound offensive tackle, played with the Buffalo Bills and Philadelphia Eagles between 1992 and 1998.

9. STEVE COLLIER

Six-foot, seven-inch, 342-pound tackle Steve Collier played ten games for the Green Bay Packers in 1987.

10. ORLANDO BROWN

Three hundred and forty pound offensive tackle Orlando Brown has played for the Cleveland Browns and Baltimore Ravens.

MEAL TICKETS

Football players don't get that big by not eating. As evidenced by this list, they sometimes have unusual tastes.

1. CLARENCE HERSCHBERGER

Clarence Herschberger was a star halfback for the University of Chicago Maroons. Coach Amos Alonzo Stagg had his players adhere to strict training rules during the week of a game. Although the team was preparing for a game with Wisconsin, Herschberger decided to ignore Stagg's rule against excessive eating. He challenged quarterback Walter Kennedy to an eating contest. After their binge, each player had gained seven pounds. Determined to win the contest at all costs, Herschberger ate 13 eggs on the morning of the game. Suffering from gastritis, he was unable to play. Without their best runner, Chicago lost to Wisconsin by the score of 23–8. The furious coach snarled, "We weren't beaten by 11 Badgers. We were beaten by 13 eggs."

2. MERCURY MORRIS

During the 1974 season, Miami Dolphins' running back Mercury Morris was hobbled by a knee injury. He resented it when coach Don Shula wanted him to run back kickoffs. Afraid of permanently injuring his knee, Morris decided to seek help from an unconventional source. Morris visited The Rootman, a Haitian witch doctor who lived in Miami. He asked if The Rootman could do something to change the coach's mind about using Morris on special teams. The witch doctor instructed Morris chew on roots. He put a "Don Shula" doll in a box and buried it. On the day of the big game against the Oakland Raiders, Morris chewed more roots. On a piece of paper he drew a spider web and wrote "Confused" on it. Whether the voodoo worked is a matter of opinion, but coach Shula was not at his best, and the two-time Super Bowl champion Dolphins lost to the Raiders. More importantly, Shula forgot to have Mercury Morris return kicks.

3. GRANT TEAFF

Baylor was given little chance of defeating Texas in their 1978 meeting. The Bears, coached by Grant Teaff, were 2–8 going into the game. In an attempt to inspire his players, he gave an unusual pep talk. He told his players a story about Eskimos ice fishing. One Eskimo pulled a worm from his mouth. "The key to success is to keep the worms warm," he explained. To prove his point, Coach Teaff ate a worm. It's unclear if the demonstration inspired the players or just grossed them out. Whatever the case, Baylor upset the Longhorns 38–13.

4. ART DONOVAN

Art Donovan was a Hall of Fame defensive tackle with the great Baltimore Colts teams of the 1950s. The only thing he did better than play football was eat. He claimed he could eat 25 to 50 hot dogs at one sitting. His diet consisted of

Spam, cheeseburgers, and pizza. Donovan confessed, "I'm a light eater. I never start eating until it gets light." The Colts wrote a stipulation in his contract that he be fined $1,000 if he broke 270 pounds. Every Friday he was weighed. Donovan would do a striptease on the scale, peeling off every bit of clothing, then go on an eating binge after the weigh-in. He would have to starve himself from Monday through Friday to lose the weight. Donovan's autobiography was titled *Fatso.*

5. **HOLLYWOOD HENDERSON**

One of the game's biggest hot dogs, Henderson once threw a tantrum over missing hot dogs. During his final NFL season with the Houston Oilers in 1980, Henderson requested that he have two hot dogs placed in his locker at halftime. The team's equipment manager found the frankfurters and ate them. Upon discovering the theft, Henderson demanded that the stadium security guards fill out a missing hot dog report. When he learned the identity of the thief, he chased the culprit all over the field.

6. **DAVE CASPER**

One of the best tight ends in NFL history, Dave Casper caught 52 touchdown passes during his 11-year career. He was playing with the Houston Oilers in the early 1980s when he devised an unconventional diet. During the team meals, he would chew his steak and potatoes and then spit them out. Scraps of undigested food dangled from the face-mask of his helmet. Casper reasoned that by chewing the food without swallowing it, he could get the nutrients without taking in the calories.

7. BOB ST. CLAIR

Bob "The Geek" St. Clair was a six-foot, nine-inch offensive tackle for the San Francisco Forty-Niners from 1953 to 1963. The three-time All Pro liked to eat raw meat, especially liver.

8. GEORGE ALLEN

An outstanding head coach with the Los Angeles Rams and Washington Redskins from 1966 to 1977, George Allen's record was 116 wins, 47 losses, and 5 ties. Rarely did he not think about football. Once he was having lunch at a golf course with quarterback Roman Gabriel when he conceived of a new defense. On his plate he cut up a piece of roast beef to represent the offense and aligned the peas in a defensive formation.

9. RUSTY TILLMAN

Rusty Tillman, a linebacker with the Washington Redskins from 1970 to 1977, dated Susan Ford, the daughter of President Gerald Ford. At Susan's birthday party, several of Tillman's teammates, including quarterback Billy Kilmer and safety Jake Scott, got into a food fight with secret service men. The secret service agents returned to the White House with their suits covered in birthday cake.

10. ALLAN SACHS

In 1974, Allan Sachs of the Minnesota Meat Company traded a hindquarter of beef for a season ticket to the Minnesota Vikings.

DRINKING IT ALL IN

Not all football players drink Gatorade.

1. OORANG INDIANS

The Oorang Indians may not have been the best team in NFL history, but they were certainly the thirstiest. On the eve of a game in Chicago, several Oorang players were angered when a bartender tried to close his saloon. They locked him in a telephone booth and drank until dawn. The next day the hung-over team was clobbered by the Bears. On another occasion, in St. Louis, the players stayed out so late that they missed the last trolley. The drunken teammates hijacked a trolley heading in the opposite direction, lifted it off the tracks, and turned it around.

2. PACKER FAN

During Vince Lombardi's first season as coach of Green Bay in 1958, the Packers were playing at home against San Francisco. When no one was looking, an unknown Packer fan spiked the

Forty-Niners' water bucket with scotch. The plan backfired as the tipsy Forty-Niners defeated the Packers 33–12.

3. FRANK MASON

On November 28, 1907, Mississippi played rival Mississippi State in a Thanksgiving contest. Ole Miss coach Frank Mason secretly laced his team's coffee with whiskey in an attempt to keep his players warm. The soused players lost 15–0, but didn't seem too upset by the outcome.

4. DOUG ATKINS

At six feet, eight inches tall, Doug Atkins was an imposing sight. The All-Pro defensive end played for the Chicago Bears from 1955 to 1966. Atkins was so strong that he once threw an offensive lineman at the quarterback. In one game the Bears trailed by 14 points at halftime. Coach George Halas was not in a good mood, and he was infuriated when he saw Atkins drinking a soda pop. Soft drinks were prohibited until after the game. Halas asked Atkins to put down the soft drink, but his request was ignored. The 70-year-old coach tried to wrestle the bottle away from the 275-pound lineman. The men fought over the pop for several minutes, stopping only when the Bears had to return to the field for the second half. When Chicago rallied for a comeback victory, a reporter asked what kind of rousing halftime speech Halas had delivered to inspire his team.

5. JOHNNY BLOOD

Johnny Blood, a halfback with the Green Bay Packers during the early 1930s, had a well-publicized penchant for alcohol.

Coach Curley Lambeau even offered Blood more money if he would give up drinking, but to no avail. After one game, Blood called room service at the Victoria Hotel and asked for ice to put in his mixed drinks. When room service didn't respond, Blood went out and bought a 100-pound cake of ice which he placed in the bathtub.

6. JOE KUHARICH

In 1950, Joe Kuharich, coach of the University of San Francisco, had his team practice in the desert in Corning, California. Practicing in temperatures over 100 degrees, players were constantly drinking water. To discourage this, Kuharich added oatmeal to the water bucket.

7. TED HENDRICKS

The Oakland Raiders held their training camp in the Sonoma Valley in the heart of California wine country. Between workouts, linebacker Ted Hendricks and lineman John Matuszak once visited a nearby winery. Hendricks returned to practice with purple teeth.

8. JOHN HEISMAN

The legendary college coach for whom the Heisman Trophy is named had unusual ideas about what his players should drink or eat. He believed that hot water weakened people and forbade anyone from drinking coffee or eating hot soup. Other prohibited foods included apple pie and peanuts. Oddly, he encouraged the consumption of raw meat.

9. GINO MARCHETTI

One of the greatest defensive ends in pro football history, Gino Marchetti starred for the Baltimore Colts from 1953 to

1966. He and fellow lineman Art Donovan would down a dozen beers each while watching Raymond Berry run pass patterns after practice.

10. **RED GRANGE**

Superstar players often endorse products. One of the strangest was Red Grange's endorsement of yeast-foam malted milk.

MAKING PASSES

Traditionally, the head cheerleader dates the star quarterback. Football heroes have always been attractive to the opposite sex. The men on this list never had trouble scoring on the field or off.

1. JOE NAMATH

Joe Namath was a prized prospect from the time he played quarterback for Beaver Falls High School in Pennsylvania. Offered scholarships by more than fifty colleges, Namath visited the Notre Dame campus at South Bend, Indiana. He was informed that there were no coeds, but there was an all-girls' college nearby. Namath replied, "I can't waste my time telephoning girls. I want to play where the girls are." Namath decided to attend the University of Alabama. His reputation as football's most eligible bachelor only increased during his tenure as "Broadway" Joe Namath of the New York Jets.

2. SHIPWRECK KELLY

Known as the "Fastest Man in the South," John "Shipwreck" Kelly was an All-American halfback at the University of Kentucky. As a professional, he led the NFL in receptions in

1933. Kelly was not your average pro football player though. He lived in an 18-room mansion on Long Island Sound worthy of Jay Gatsby. The home included trophies from safaris around the world—mounted heads of lions and tigers, skins of leopards, cheetahs, and jaguars. Photos in the home documented his remarkable array of friends. He played golf with the Duke of Windsor and visited Aristotle Onassis in the south of France. Kelly went to a bullfight with painter Pablo Picasso. He hunted mountain lions with actor Clark Gable in Idaho and went on an African safari with author Ernest Hemingway. Among his circle of friends were Richard Nixon, Fred Astaire, Bob Hope, Bing Crosby, Casey Stengel, Maria Callas, and millionaires Jock Whitney and Dan Topping. A favorite of New York café society, Kelly was a regular at the famed nightclubs The Stork Club, 21, and El Morocco. Not surprisingly, he attracted many famous and beautiful women. His dates included actress Tallulah Bankhead, celebrated debutante Brenda Frazier, and numerous starlets.

3. O.J. SIMPSON

Buffalo running back O.J. Simpson led the NFL in rushing four times between 1972 and 1976 and was the first professional player to rush for more than 2,000 yards in a season. With movie-star looks, Simpson never had any problem attracting beautiful women. Over the years he dated many models and actresses, including a reported fling with actress Tawny Kitaen.

4. FRANK GIFFORD

Frank Gifford scored 78 touchdowns during his Hall of Fame career with the New York Giants, which lasted from 1952 to 1964. The handsome Gifford's first wife was a homecoming queen. His second wife, Kathie Lee Gifford, is a popular television personality. Their marriage took a hit when Frank, in his mid-sixties, was caught on film having sex with a buxom blonde in a hotel room.

5. GEORGE PRESTON MARSHALL

George Preston Marshall owned the Washington Redskins from 1939 to 1969. The millionaire had made his fortune in the laundry business. He married silent-film actress Corinne Griffith. Marshall also had a long-term, passionate affair with actress Louise Brooks, one of the most beautiful stars ever to appear in film. Although Brooks had relationships with many famous men, including Charlie Chaplin, she confessed that George Preston Marshall was the love of her life.

6. JOHNNY BLOOD

Johnny Blood, the Hall of Fame halfback, was known as a ladies man. It was said that he once paid a madam for the services of every prostitute in a brothel.

7. PAUL HORNUNG

Paul Hornung became a gridiron idol during his days as a Heisman Trophy winner at Notre Dame. Nicknamed the "Golden Boy" because of his curly blonde hair, Hornung made women swoon with his good looks. As a rookie with the Green Bay Packers in 1957, he dated Hollywood starlets. Once, during a game against the Los Angeles Rams, a stunning brunette came out of the stands to have her photo taken with Hornung.

8. BOB WATERFIELD

A two-time NFL Most Valuable Player, quarterback Bob Waterfield played for the Rams from 1945 to 1952. In 1943, he married Jane Russell, who became one of Hollywood's biggest sex symbols.

9. MARK GASTINEAU

In 1984, New York Jets' defensive end Mark Gastineau set an NFL record with 22 sacks. He had a highly publicized relationship with actress Brigitte Nielsen, former wife of Sylvester Stallone.

10. GLENN DAVIS

Army halfback Glenn Davis won the Heisman Trophy in 1946. In the late 1940s, Davis dated young actress Elizabeth Taylor.

ONE-GAME WONDERS

On September 27, 1953, kicker Bert Rechichar of the Baltimore Colts had the game of his life. Rechichar accounted for all the points in a 13–9 victory over the Chicago Bears. In the second quarter, Rechichar, playing defensive back, intercepted a pass and returned it 35 yards for a touchdown. On the final play of the first half, Rechichar kicked a 56-yard field goal, the longest in NFL history at the time. The record lasted until 1970, when Tom Dempsey kicked his historic 63-yard field goal. Rechichar kicked only 31 field goals in 89 attempts during his ten-year career. Like Rechichar, these otherwise ordinary players each had one outstanding game to remember.

1. CLINT LONGLEY

Subbing for injured Dallas quarterback Roger Staubach, Clint Longley was an unlikely hero in a 1974 Thanksgiving Day game against the Washington Redskins. The rookie from Abilene Christian threw two touchdown passes in leading the Cowboys to a 24–23 victory over the Redskins. Longley threw only three more touchdown passes during the remainder of his three-year career.

2. PERCY HOWARD

Rookie wide receiver Percy Howard never caught a pass in the 1975 regular season, but made a memorable reception in the Super Bowl. In the fourth quarter of Super Bowl X versus the Pittsburgh Steelers, Howard caught a 34-yard touchdown pass from Roger Staubach in a 21–17 loss. It turned out to be Howard's last game in the NFL.

3. STEVE BELICHICK

Steve Belichick fielded only one punt in his NFL career, but he made the most of it. In a 1941 game against the Green Bay Packers, the Detroit Lions' rookie ran back a punt for a 77-yard touchdown. It was his team's only score in a 24–7 loss. After the season was over, Belicheck entered the military and never played in another NFL game.

4. JOHNNY JACKSON

Johnny Jackson of the University of Houston intercepted three passes in a 60–40 win over Texas in a game played on November 7, 1987. Jackson returned the interceptions for touchdowns of 31, 53, and 97 yards. These were the only touchdowns Jackson scored in college.

5. GEORGE IZO

George Izo was a one-play wonder. On September 15, 1964, the Washington Redskins' quarterback tied an NFL record with a 99-yard touchdown pass to Bobby Mitchell in a 37–14 loss to the Cleveland Browns. It was the highlight of a mediocre career. During his seven years as a pro, Izo only threw 12 touchdown passes and had 32 passes intercepted.

6. A.J. DUHE

Miami Dolphins' linebacker A.J. Duhe intercepted three passes, one for a touchdown, in a 14–0 victory over the New York Jets in the 1982 AFC championship game. During his eight-year career, Duhe had only three other interceptions.

7. WILLIE ANDERSON

Willie "Flipper" Anderson of the Los Angeles Rams caught 15 passes for 336 yards in a 20–17 win against the New Orleans Saints on November 26, 1989. The 336 yards were the most receiving yards in a game in NFL history. Anderson never before had more than 122 yards in a game.

8. DIPPY EVANS

Fred "Dippy" Evans, a defensive back with the Chicago Bears, is the only player in NFL history to return two fumbles for touchdowns in one game. He achieved this feat on November 28, 1948, in a 48–13 victory against the Washington Redskins. His two touchdowns measured 13 and 15 yards. The fumble recoveries were the only ones of Evans' NFL career.

9. LUTHER BRADLEY

Defensive back Luther Bradley of the Chicago Blitz intercepted six passes in a United States Football League game played on April 2, 1983. The interceptions included a 93-yard touchdown as Chicago blitzed the Tampa Bay Bandits by the score of 42–3. During his four-year NFL career, Bradley had only nine interceptions.

10. ELMER ANGSMAN

Unheralded halfback Elmer Angsman of the Chicago Cardinals is the only player in NFL history to have a pair of 70-yard touchdown runs in a championship game. Angsman's two breakaway runs lifted the Cardinals to a 28–21 victory over the Philadelphia Eagles. He scored only five touchdowns during his seven-year professional career.

THE BEST YEAR OF THEIR LIVES

In the course of fairly undistinguished careers, some players have had single seasons in which they could do no wrong. Each of these players turned in one memorable year.

1. BEATTIE FEATHERS

In 1934, Beattie Feathers of the Chicago Bears had one of the greatest rookie seasons in NFL history. Feathers led the league in rushing with 1,004 yards and averaged an incredible 8.4 yards per carry, still an NFL record. Late in his rookie season, he dislocated his shoulder, and he played the rest of his career in an immobilizing brace. In his final six seasons, Feathers rushed for only 976 yards.

2. RICKY BELL

The first player selected in the 1977 NFL draft, Tampa Bay Buccaneers running back Ricky Bell rushed for 1,263 yards in 1979, his best season. The total nearly doubled his previous best. In his next three seasons, Bell rushed for a total of only 685 yards.

3. DON MAJKOWSKI

Green Bay Packers' quarterback Don Majkowski led the NFL in completions (353) and passing yards (4,318) in 1989. During that season he threw 27 touchdown passes. Majkowski was never able to recreate the magic of that season. In his final seven campaigns, he threw only 25 more touchdown passes.

4. BUCKY POPE

Rookie sensation Bucky Pope averaged 31.4 yards per catch with the Los Angeles Rams in 1964. That year he led all receivers with ten touchdowns. Pope caught only nine passes in his final three seasons.

5. STEVE OWENS

In 1971, his first full season, Detroit Lions' running back Steve Owens rushed for more than 1,000 yards. Plagued by injuries, the former Heisman Trophy winner rushed for fewer than 1,300 yards for the remainder of his career.

6. BARRY FOSTER

In 1992, Pittsburgh Steelers' running back Barry Foster had a fantastic season. Foster rushed for 1,690 yards and scored 11 touchdowns. Foster never came close to duplicating his success and was out of the league by 1995.

7. ANTHONY JOHNSON

During his first six seasons, running back Anthony Johnson rushed for a total of 1,169 yards. In 1996, with the Carolina Panthers, Johnson rushed for 1,120 yards. The next season his total dropped to 358.

8. DAVID SIMS

Seattle Seahawks' running back David Sims led the NFL in touchdowns in 1978 with fifteen. He rushed for 752 yards and caught 30 passes. The next season, his last in the NFL, Sims rushed for only 53 yards.

9. JACK THOMPSON

The Cincinnati Bengals thought Jack Thompson was their quarterback of the future when they drafted him in the first round in 1979. After four disappointing seasons in Cincinnati, the "Throwin' Samoan" lived up to his potential by passing for nearly 3,000 yards and 18 touchdowns for Tampa Bay in 1983. The following season, his last, Thompson threw only two touchdown passes.

10. DON SANDIFER

Defensive back Don Sandifer led the NFL in interceptions as a rookie with the Washington Redskins in 1948. His 13 interceptions was an NFL record. In his final five seasons, Sandifer picked off only ten more passes.

THE ONE AND ONLY

The following individuals are one-of-a-kinds.

1. ALDO DONELLI

Aldo Donelli holds the distinction of being the only man to coach an NFL team and a college football team simultaneously. In 1941, Donelli was the coach of the Pittsburgh Steelers. At the same time he served as head coach of the Duquesne University football team. After his Steelers lost their first five games, Donelli quit to coach college football full time. The move paid off as Duquesne finished the season undefeated.

2. HUGO BEZDEK

The only man to manage a major-league baseball team and coach an NFL team was Hugo Bezdek. Born in Czechoslovakia, Bezdek managed baseball's Pittsburgh Pirates from 1917 to 1919. He coached the Cleveland Rams to a 1–13 record during the 1937 and 1938 seasons.

3. ARCHIE GRIFFIN

The only player to win the Heisman Trophy twice was Ohio State running back Archie Griffin. He won the award as the nation's outstanding college football player in 1974 and 1975. Griffin rushed for more than 100 yards 31 consecutive games and finished his career as a Buckeye with 5,177 yards.

4. FRANK REICH

The only quarterback to lead a professional team to victory from a 32-point deficit was Buffalo's Frank Reich. With starting quarterback Jim Kelly on the sidelines with a knee injury, Reich and the Bills trailed the Houston Oilers 35–3 in the third quarter of their playoff game on January 3, 1993. Reich threw three touchdown passes to Andre Reed as the Bills rallied to a thrilling 41–38 victory. In college, Reich led Maryland to the biggest comeback in college football history in a game against Miami of Florida.

5. OTTO GRAHAM

Otto Graham is the only pro quarterback to lead his team to ten consecutive championship games. Graham was the quarterback for the Cleveland Browns from 1946 to 1955, and every season they reached the title game. The Browns were victorious in seven of those games.

6. WEEB EUBANK

The only coach to win championships in both the NFL and AFL was Weeb Eubank. His Baltimore Colts won NFL titles in 1958 and 1959. Eubank later coached the New York Jets to the AFL title in 1968. His Jets upset the Baltimore Colts 16–7 in Super Bowl III.

7. MIKE WILSON

Offensive lineman Mike Wilson is the only man to play in five different professional football leagues. In 1969, Wilson played with the Cincinnati Bengals of the American Football League. Wilson then played for the Buffalo Bills and Kansas City Chiefs of the National Football League. Next, he was a member of the Detroit Wheels of the World Football League in 1974. Between 1976 and 1980, Wilson played in the Canadian Football League. Wilson's final team was the 1983 Los Angeles Express in the United States Football League.

8. LARRY BALL

Linebacker Larry Ball is the only player to be on the rosters of undefeated and winless teams in the NFL. As a rookie, he played with the 1972 Miami Dolphins that won all 17 games en route to a Super Bowl Championship. Four years later, Ball suffered through a winless season with the expansion Tampa Bay Buccaneers.

9. LES RICHTER

Les Richter was so highly regarded that the Los Angeles Rams traded eleven players to the Dallas Texans for him. The linebacker justified their faith by being selected to eight Pro Bowls.

10. RICHARD SLIGH

Defensive tackle Richard Sligh appeared in eight games for the 1967 Oakland Raiders. What makes Sligh unique is that he was the only seven-footer to play professional football.

SIXTY-MINUTE MEN

In the early days of football, players were expected to play both offense and defense. George Halas once described Red Grange as "the game's greatest runner and defensive back." Even in the last twenty years, players such as Deion Sanders and Roy Green have excelled at both offense and defense. These athletes played with distinction on both sides of the ball.

1. SAMMY BAUGH

Sammy Baugh threw 187 touchdown passes and is regarded as one of the greatest quarterbacks in football history. Baugh was also a brilliant defensive back and a record-setting punter. In the 1936 Sugar Bowl, played in a driving rainstorm, he almost single-handedly led Texas Christian to a 3–2 victory over Louisiana State University. In addition to his pinpoint passing, Baugh had a 42-yard run. Despite the poor footing, he punted for a 48-yard average. On defense, he intercepted two passes and made eight tackles, including an open field game saver. As a professional with the Washington Redskins, Baugh set over a dozen passing records. In 1943, he led NFL defensive backs with 11 interceptions. On November 14, 1943, Baugh threw four touchdown passes and intercepted four passes in a 42–20 win against the Detroit Lions. In 1940, Baugh set a record which still stands when he averaged 51.4 yards per punt.

2. CHUCK BEDNARIK

Chuck Bednarik was the ultimate sixty-minute player. The eight-time Pro Bowler starred for the Philadelphia Eagles from 1949 to 1962. Bednarik is not only rated one of the best linebackers in NFL history, but also one of the greatest centers to play the game.

3. BILL DUDLEY

An All-American who played at the University of Virginia, "Bullet" Bill Dudley scored eighteen touchdowns in 1941. The running back was an immediate success as a pro, winning the rushing title as a rookie with the Pittsburgh Steelers in 1942. Four years later Dudley not only led the NFL in rushing, but he paced the league in interceptions with ten. Named the NFL's Most Valuable Player in 1946, he was also tops in punt return yardage as well.

4. BULLDOG TURNER

Clyde "Bulldog" Turner could play any position except quarterback. Primarily a center, the seven-time All-Pro also was an exceptional linebacker. In 1942, he became the only linebacker in NFL history to lead the league in interceptions.

5. LEO NOMELLINI

Hall of Famer Leo Nomellini played both defensive and offensive tackle for the San Francisco Forty-Niners. He was selected All-NFL twice as an offensive tackle and four times as a defensive tackle.

6. DON HUTSON

Until the emergence of Jerry Rice, Don Hutson was regarded as the greatest receiver in NFL history. He led the league in receptions eight times and scored 105 touchdowns for the Green Bay Packers between 1935 and 1945. A skilled pass defender, Hutson led the league in interceptions in 1940.

7. GEORGE CONNOR

George Connor played guard, offensive tackle, defensive tackle, and linebacker for the Chicago Bears between 1948 and 1955. From 1951 through 1953, Connor was selected an All-Pro on both offense and defense.

8. LEROY KEYES

An All-American at Purdue, Leroy Keyes played defensive back, running back, and flanker. Keyes finished second in the 1968 Heisman Trophy balloting to O.J. Simpson. In his five-year professional career with the Philadelphia Eagles and Kansas City Chiefs, Keyes played both running back and defensive back.

9. MEL HEIN

During his fifteen-year career with the New York Giants, Mel Hein played every minute of every game. The Most Valuable Player of the NFL in 1938, Hein was a star center on offense and linebacker on defense.

10. GLENN DAVIS

Glenn Davis of Army was one of the best halfbacks in college football history. In 1946, Davis had his greatest all-around game in a 20–13 victory over Michigan. Davis rushed for 105 yards, including a 58-yard touchdown. He completed all seven passes for 159 yards and a touchdown. On defense, he intercepted two passes and made the game-saving tackle.

YOU CAN LOOK IT UP: COLLEGE

College football records aren't always set by Heisman Trophy winners or players who go on to greatness as professionals. Most records belong to little-known athletes. For example, Jarrod De Georgia of Wayne State completed fifty-six passes in a game against Drake on November 9, 1996. Chris Bisaillon had fifty-five touchdown receptions for Illinois Wesleyan between 1989 and 1992.

1. LEO SCHLICK

Halfback Leo Schlick of St. Viator College (Indiana) scored 100 points in a 1916 game, a feat that has never been duplicated. His point total included 12 touchdowns.

2. DAVID KLINGLER

Houston quarterback David Klingler set numerous major college passing records. In 1990, he threw 54 touchdown passes and passed for 5,140 yards. In a 62–45 victory over Arizona State on December 2, 1990, he passed for 716 yards. On August 31, 1991, Klingler threw six touchdown passes in a quarter versus Louisiana Tech. He set another

Jon SooHoo

David Klingler

Quarterback David Klingler set numerous college passing records and once threw 54 touchdown passes in a single season for the University of Houston. The Cincinnati Bengals drafted him with the seventh overall pick in 1992, but he was a flop at the professional level.

record when he tossed 11 touchdown passes in an 84–21 romp over Eastern Michigan on November 17, 1990.

3. BRIAN SHAY

Running back Brian Shay of Emporia State (Illinois) rushed for a college record 6,958 yards during his career from 1995 to 1998. Shay averaged nearly seven yards per carry during his college career. He also set college records by scoring 88 touchdowns and 544 points.

4. FORREST PETERS

Montana State freshman Forrest Peters set a record which would make any kicker envious. In a 1924 game Peters kicked 17 field goals.

5. DENNIS SHAW

San Diego State quarterback Dennis Shaw threw seven touchdown passes in the first half of a 70–21 victory over New Mexico on November 15, 1969. Shaw finished the game with nine touchdown passes and 441 passing yards. His favorite receiver, Tom Delaney, caught six touchdown passes. Backup quarterback Brian Sipe, who went on to become an NFL star, came in late in the game and threw a tenth touchdown pass for the Aztecs.

6. WILLIE TOTTEN

Mississippi Valley quarterback Willie Totten set a Division I-AA passing record with 56 touchdown passes in 1984. Many of his passes were caught by future NFL great Jerry Rice.

7. RANDY GATEWOOD

Wide receiver Randy Gatewood of the University of Nevada at Las Vegas caught 23 passes for 363 yards in a game against Idaho on September 17, 1994.

8. BILL BORCHERT

Quarterback Bill Borchert of Mount Union College threw a record 141 touchdown passes from 1994 to 1997. During that time he completed 671 passes while throwing only 17 interceptions.

9. DANTE BROWN

Only a handful of running backs have rushed for more than 400 yards in a game. The only player to do it twice was Dante Brown of Marietta College. On October 5, 1996, he gained 441 yards in a game against Baldwin College. Five weeks later he rushed for 413 yards in a game with Heidelberg.

10. SCOTT PINGEL

Scott Pingel, a wide receiver for Westminster College (Missouri) caught 130 passes for 2,157 yards and 26 touchdowns in 1998. In his best game, he gained 395 yards against Bethel on November 7, 1998.

YOU CAN LOOK IT UP: PRO

Not every professional football record was set by Dan Marino or Walter Payton. Here are some notable achievements by players who are not so well publicized.

1. DON CURRIVAN

Who's the only wide receiver in National Football League history to average over 25 yards per reception for an entire career? If you answered Don Currivan, you are correct. During his pro career, which lasted from 1943 to 1949, Currivan averaged 25.4 yards per catch. In 1947, while playing for the Boston Yanks, Currivan caught 24 passes for 782 yards, an incredible 32.6 yards per reception.

2. STEVE O'NEAL

Steve O'Neal never led the NFL in punting, but on September 21, 1969, the New York Jets rookie kicked the perfect punt in a game against the Denver Broncos. From his own end zone, O'Neal boomed a punt that travelled more than 70 yards in the air. Landing at the Broncos' 30-yard line, it bounced and rolled dead at the Denver one. The 98-yard punt is a National Football League record. Despite the perfect punt, the Jets lost the game 21–19.

3. AL NELSON

Defensive back Al Nelson played for the Philadelphia Eagles from 1965 to 1973. Nelson has the distinction of being the only player to return two missed field goals 100 yards for touchdowns. On December 11, 1966, Nelson returned a missed field goal 100 yards in a 33–21 victory over the Cleveland Browns. Five years later, he returned a missed field goal attempt by the Pittsburgh Steelers 101 yards in a 30–27 loss.

4. TOMMY O'CONNELL

An 18th-round draft choice by the Chicago Bears in 1952, quarterback Tommy O'Connell experienced a career year with the Cleveland Browns in 1957. He set an NFL record when he averaged 11.17 yards per pass. After his record-setting season, he never played another game in the National Football League.

5. TOM FEARS

Los Angeles Rams' end Tom Fears led the National Football League in receptions during his first three seasons. On December 3, 1950, Fears set a record when he caught 18 passes in a 54–14 victory over the Green Bay Packers. Fears caught ten passes in the fourth quarter alone.

6. DON HULTZ

Defensive lineman Don Hultz played for the Minnesota Vikings, Philadelphia Eagles, and Chicago Bears from 1963 to 1974. As a rookie with the Vikings in 1963, Hultz set a single-season record with nine fumble recoveries. He recovered only three fumbles in his final ten years.

7. JOE FERGUSON

In 1975, Joe Ferguson of the Buffalo Bills led the NFL in touchdown passes with 25. The following season he set a record when he threw only one interception in 151 attempts.

8. BOBBY DOUGLASS

As a pro passer, Bobby Douglass was nothing special. He threw only 36 touchdown passes during his ten-year career. However, Douglass was unsurpassed as a running quarterback. In 1972, with the Chicago Bears, Douglass rushed for 968 yards, a record for quarterbacks. He led all rushers with a 6.9 yards-per-attempt average that year.

9. OTTO GRAHAM

No quarterback in NFL history has averaged more yards per pass attempt in a career than Cleveland's Otto Graham. He averaged 8.63 yards per pass for the Browns from 1950 to 1955. His best season was 1953 when he averaged more than ten-and-a-half yards per attempt.

10. JERRY NORTON

Jerry Norton led the National Football League with ten interceptions in 1960. The St. Louis Cardinals' defensive back is the only player to intercept four passes in a game on two occasions. Norton intercepted four passes on November 20, 1960, in a 26–14 victory over the Washington Redskins. A year later, he repeated the feat in a 30–27 loss to Pittsburgh.

RECORDS WHICH MAY NEVER BE BROKEN

It's said that records are meant to be broken, but some of these milestones may never be surpassed.

1. BEATTIE FEATHERS

Rookie running back Beattie Feathers of the Chicago Bears led the National Football League in rushing in 1934 with 1,004 yards. He averaged 8.4 yards per carry, a record that still stands.

2. GEORGE BLANDA

Quarterback and place kicker George Blanda set a record for longevity that may never be equalled. Blanda played in the National Football League from 1949 to 1958. He retired in 1959 because the Chicago Bears were only interested in his services as a kicker. The following season he signed with the Houston Oilers of the American Football League and enjoyed his greatest years at quarterback. By the time he retired for good in 1976, George Blanda had played 26 seasons as a professional.

3. PAUL KRAUSE

As a rookie with the Washington Redskins in 1964, defensive back Paul Krause led the NFL with 12 interceptions. By the time he retired in 1979, Krause had intercepted a record 81 passes.

4. NIGHT TRAIN LANE

Dick "Night Train" Lane, a rookie defensive back with the Los Angeles Rams, set a single-season record when he intercepted 14 passes in 1952. Lane also led the league in interceptions in 1954.

5. TOM MORROW

Defensive back Tom Morrow of the Oakland Raiders intercepted passes in eight consecutive games. The streak began in 1962 and continued into the 1963 season. Because the interception rates have dropped significantly in recent years, the interception records of Paul Krause, Night Train Lane, and Tom Morrow appear to be safe.

6. TRAVIS WILLIAMS

During his rookie season in 1967, Green Bay Packers' kick return specialist Travis Williams averaged an amazing 41.1 yards per return. Williams ran back four of his 18 returns for touchdowns.

7. SAMMY BAUGH

In 1940, Sammy Baugh of the Washington Redskins averaged 51.3 yards per punt. With the modern punter's emphasis on hang time instead of distance, Baugh's record should stand for at least another 60 years.

Jon SooHoo

Dan Marino

Marino's powerful arm and quick-release throw helped make him the most prolific passer in NFL history.

8. JOHNNY UNITAS

Of the many records established by the Baltimore Colts' Johnny Unitas, the one that still stands is his mark for consecutive games in which he threw a touchdown pass. From 1956 to 1960, Unitas had at least one touchdown pass in 47 consecutive games.

9. DAN MARINO

The man who now owns most of the NFL passing records is Dan Marino. In 1984, Marino threw 48 touchdown passes for the Miami Dolphins. Only one other quarterback in National Football League history, Kurt Warner, has ever thrown more than 40 touchdown passes in a season.

10. THE 1934 DETROIT LIONS

One of the most unbreakable team records belongs to the 1934 Detroit Lions. The Lions shut out their first seven opponents. Their defense was so dominant that no team was able to penetrate their 20-yard line. Detroit won its first ten games, only to lose its final three.

THE WORST PLAYS OF ALL TIME

A lot can go wrong on a football field. See what can happen when a play goes awry.

1. ROY RIEGELS

Roy "Wrong Way" Riegels of the University of California earned his nickname in the 1929 Rose Bowl against Georgia Tech. In the second quarter of a scoreless tie, Riegels scooped up a fumble by Stumpy Thomason at the Georgia Tech 35-yard line. Riegels got turned around when he swerved to avoid a tackler. To the horror of his teammates, he began to run the wrong way. Just as he was about to cross the goal line, he was caught by teammate Benny Lom who turned him in the right direction. At that moment he was tackled by Georgia Tech players at the one-yard line. A few plays later, Georgia Tech blocked a punt for a safety. The two points proved the difference as Georgia Tech defeated California 8–7.

2. JIM MARSHALL

Minnesota Vikings' defensive end Jim Marshall provided the pro equivalent to Roy Riegels' wrong way run in an October 25, 1964, game against the San Francisco Forty-Niners.

Marshall picked up a fumble by San Francisco's Bill Kilmer in the fourth quarter and began running toward the wrong goal line. After completing his 60-yard run for what he thought was a touchdown, Marshall jubilantly tossed the ball out of the end zone. Only when San Francisco center Bruce Bosley congratulated him did Marshall realize his mistake. Luckily, the safety did not prove costly as the Vikings held on to a 27–22 win.

3. JOE PISARCIK

In a play remembered bitterly by New York fans as "The Fumble," the Giants turned a sure victory into a defeat. The Giants led the Philadelphia Eagles 17–12 with time running out in a game played on November 19, 1978. With third down, two yards to go, and no time outs remaining for the Eagles, all New York quarterback Joe Pisarcik had to do was take the snap, kneel down, and the game would be over. Incredibly, a play was sent in from the sidelines to hand off to running back Larry Csonka. Pisarcik mishandled the ball and Philadelphia's Herman Edwards picked it up and ran 26 yards for the winning touchdown. As a result of calling the ill-advised play, offensive coordinator Bob Gibson was fired.

4. SAM WYCHE

Cincinnati Bengals head coach Sam Wyche showed that a team didn't have to fumble in the final seconds to lose a game. Wyche's Bengals were leading the San Francisco Forty-Niners 26–20 with six seconds remaining in a game played on September 20, 1987. On fourth down everyone in Riverfront Stadium expected the Bengals to punt the ball. Wyche had other ideas and called for a handoff to running back James Brooks, who was tackled at his own 25-yard line with two seconds remaining on the clock. On the final play of the game, San Francisco quarterback Joe Montana connected with receiver Jerry Rice for the tying touchdown. Ray Wersching's point after touchdown gave the Forty-Niners an unexpected victory.

5. **JIM HOGAN**

Central Florida punter Jim Hogan bowed out on a low note in his final college game against Samford on November 15, 1986. With his team comfortably ahead 66–0 in the fourth quarter, Hogan decided to show his appreciation to all of his fans. After he was hiked the ball, Hogan bowed in all four directions. Because of his showboating, the punt was blocked and recovered for Samford's only touchdown. Fearful of his coach's wrath, Hogan left the field before the game was over.

6. **JAY ESTABROOK**

Tufts' Jay Estabrook may hold the dubious distinction of making the worst kick of all time. During an October 29, 1965, game against Amherst, a strong gust of wind blew Estabrook's punt back toward him. Estabrook caught his own punt and was tackled for a four-yard loss. Amherst won the game 28–6.

7. **PHIL BUNNELL**

Indecision cost Yale a chance at victory in a November 21, 1925, game against Harvard. With seconds remaining in a scoreless tie, Yale had the ball at the Harvard one-yard line. Quarterback Phil Bunnell and captain Johnny Joss argued about what play to call. While they were discussing whether to go for a touchdown or kick a field goal, time ran out and the game ended in a tie.

8. KEN STABLER

Alabama quarterback Ken Stabler lost track of the downs and as a result cost his team an almost certain victory against Tennessee on November 16, 1965. The Crimson Tide had the ball at the Volunteers' four-yard line with time for one more play. Instead of going for a touchdown, Stabler intentionally threw the ball out of bounds to stop the clock. The only problem was that it was fourth down and Tennessee took over possession on downs. Thanks to Stabler's mental error, Tennessee escaped with a tie.

9. GARO YEPREMIAN

Kicker Garo Yepremian's miscue nearly cost the 1972 Miami Dolphins their perfect season. The Dolphins entered Super Bowl VII against the Washington Redskins with a perfect 16–0 record. With two minutes left in the game, Miami was ahead 14–0 as Yepremian prepared for a 42-yard field goal attempt. The kick was blocked and bounced right back into Yepremian's hands. Yepremian inexplicably threw a pass that was picked off by Washington's Mike Bass, who returned it 49 yards for a touchdown. Yepremian avoided becoming a goat when Miami held on for a 14–7 victory to preserve their perfect season.

10. BOB GRIESE

A year before Yepremian's folly, Miami quarterback Bob Griese had his own misadventure in Super Bowl VI against the Dallas Cowboys. Chased by Dallas linemen Bob Lilly and Jethro Pugh, Griese kept backtracking. After zigzagging all over the field, Griese was pulled down by Lilly for a 29-yard loss. The Dolphins lost the game 24–3.

THE OFFENSE RESTS

Check out some of the most dismal offensive performances in National Football League history.

1. JOHN MCCARTHY

In 1944, the National Football League combined two of its weakest teams, The Chicago Cardinals and the Pittsburgh Steelers, as part of wartime austerity. The quarterback of that team was a rookie named John McCarthy. During the season he completed only 20 passes and his completion rate was less than 30 percent. McCarthy threw 13 interceptions without a single touchdown pass. He wasn't much of a rusher either, losing 49 yards in his six attempts. The hapless team went winless and McCarthy never played in another NFL game.

2. LEW POPE

The 1934 Cincinnati Reds may have been the worst team in National Football League history. Quarterback Lew Pope's statistics for the year reflected the team's futility. Pope completed only ten of 42 passes (a 23.8-percent completion rate) for 115 yards and no touchdowns. Ten of Pope's passes were intercepted and his quarterback rating was zero. In two seasons with Cincinnati, Pope threw 12 interceptions without ever connecting for a touchdown pass.

3. WAYNE CLARK

Quarterback Wayne Clark played for the San Diego Chargers, Cincinnati Bengals, and Kansas City Chiefs from 1970 to 1974. During his five seasons, he never threw a touchdown pass in 120 attempts. Fourteen of Clark's passes were intercepted.

4. BOBBY HOYING

Philadelphia Eagles' quarterback Bobby Hoying suffered through a nightmarish season in 1998. Hoying did not throw a touchdown pass all season in 224 attempts. Opposing defenses picked off nine of his errant passes.

5. ART MICHALIK

Place kicker Art Michalik was nicknamed "Automatic Art." Considering his lack of kicking success, one wonders how he got the nickname. In 1955, the Pittsburgh Steeler connected on only one of 12 field goal attempts. While extra points are automatic to most kickers, Michalik was successful on only nine of 15 attempts.

6. BOB TIMBERLAKE

The only field goal kicker in NFL history who could match Art Michalik's record of futility was Bob Timberlake. As a rookie with the 1965 New York Giants, Timberlake kicked only one field goal in 15 attempts. Not surprisingly, Timberlake was given the boot by the Giants.

7. **IRV COMP**

Quarterback Irv Comp of the Green Bay Packers led the National Football League in passing yardage in 1944. While he was a competent passer, his rushing left much to be desired. During the 1946 season, Comp gained only 62 yards in 61 attempts, a rushing average of little more than one yard per carry.

8. **JULIE AFONSE**

Tailback Julie Afonse was a dangerous receiver, averaging almost 23 yards per reception during his first two seasons in Cleveland. However, he was no breakaway threat as a rusher. In 1938, his final season, he averaged only one yard a carry in 16 attempts. His career rushing average was a poor 1.6 yards per carry.

9. **SCOTT BULL**

For three seasons Scott Bull was a quarterback for the San Francisco Forty-Niners. In 1978, his final season, Bull threw only one touchdown pass in 16 games while allowing 11 interceptions. His quarterback rating for the season was a dismal 24.8. The next season the Forty-Niners drafted a quarterback to replace Bull. His name was Joe Montana.

10. **GEORGE BLANDA**

Even great players can have terrible years. In 1961, George Blanda of the Houston Oilers led American Football League quarterbacks with 36 touchdown passes. The following season Blanda threw 42 interceptions, an all-time professional record.

LOSING'S THE ONLY THING

Vince Lombardi, the personification of a winning professional football coach, said, "Winning isn't everything. It's the only thing." For every winner there has to be a loser. In his only season as a head coach in the NFL, Rod Rust led the 1990 New England Patriots to a 1–15 record. Marty Feldman—the coach, not the comedian—compiled a 2–15 record with the 1961–1962 Oakland Raiders. Joe Bugel, the coach of the Phoenix Cardinals and Oakland Raiders between 1990 and 1997, never had a winning season and compiled a 24–56 record. Here are ten more of the NFL's least successful coaches.

1. FAYE ABBOTT

During his first season as coach, Faye Abbott's 1928 Dayton Triangles lost all seven of their games. The next season the Triangles lost every game and dropped out of the National Football League. Abbott's lifetime record as an NFL coach was 0–13.

2. ALGY CLARK

Algy Clark's only season as an NFL head coach was with the 1934 Cincinnati Reds, possibly the worst team in league history. Clark's team lost all eight of their games and scored only ten points all season.

3. BILL PETERSON

Bill Peterson's debut as head coach of the 1972 Houston Oilers was less than spectacular. His Oilers lost 13 of their 14 games and were outscored during the season 447–199. After losing the first five games of the 1973 season, Peterson was fired.

4. PHIL HANDLER

As a rookie head coach with the 1943 Chicago Cardinals, Phil Handler guided his team to a 0–10 record. The Cardinals and Pittsburgh Steelers were combined in 1944. Handler served as co-coach with Walt Kiesling and once again his team went 0–10. Handler's 1945 Cardinals improved to 1–9, meaning that his teams had lost 29 of their first 30 games. His career record as an NFL head coach was four wins and 34 losses.

5. HARVEY JOHNSON

Harvey Johnson had two stints as head coach of the Buffalo Bills. In 1968, Johnson's Bills won one and lost ten. Three years later, Johnson returned to coach Buffalo to a 1–13 record.

6. MIKE NIXON

Richard Nixon wasn't the only Nixon to experience problems in Washington. Mike Nixon coached the Redskins to a combined record of 4–18–2 from 1959 to 1960. After he coached the 1965 Pittsburgh Steelers to a 2–12 record, NFL teams didn't have Nixon to kick around anymore.

7. JIM RINGO

Jim Ringo was a Hall of Fame center with the Green Bay Packers from 1963 to 1973. When the Buffalo Bills tapped him as head coach in 1976, it was hoped that some of Vince Lombardi's coaching genius had rubbed off on his player. Hired five games into the season, Ringo led the Bills to losses in their last nine games. Buffalo lost its first four games of the 1977 season en route to a 3–11 record. Ringo retired following the 1977 season with a 3–20 record as coach.

8. DAVE SHULA

If anyone had the bloodlines to be a great coach, it was Dave Shula. His father, Don Shula, is the NFL's winningest coach with 328 victories. His 1972 Miami Dolphins were the only team to win all 17 of its games. The Cincinnati Bengals were optimistic when they hired Dave Shula as head coach in 1992. During his tenure from 1992 to 1996, the Bengals never had a winning season. Shula's record as coach was 19 wins and 52 losses.

9. ABE GIBRON

Abe Gibron coached the Chicago Bears from 1972 to 1974. During that time, Gibron didn't draw any comparisons with Bears' coaching great George Halas. His teams never won more than four games in a season and his record in Chicago was a disappointing ten wins and 30 losses.

10. MARION CAMPBELL

In nine seasons as head coach of the Atlanta Falcons and Philadelphia Eagles, Marion Campbell never had a winning season. He finished his coaching career in 1989 with a record of 34 wins and 80 losses.

UNORTHODOX COACHES

Coaches motivate their players by different means. Some reward excellence on the field. Others penalize failure. The following men had their own unique coaching styles.

1. GIL DOBIE

No coach had less reason to be gloomy than Gil Dobie. In his first 11 seasons as head coach of North Dakota State and the University of Washington, Dobie's teams never lost a game. His record from 1906 to 1916 was 65 wins, no losses, and three ties. Somehow Gloomy Gil always found a way to look on the dark side. Dobie was the leading proponent of the power of negative thinking. Even though his teams rarely lost, Dobie told his teams in pre-game "pep" talks that they didn't have a chance. When informed that he had the fastest backs in the country, Dobie lamented, "That means they only get to the tacklers sooner." Asked if he was happy with his team's performance following a 49–0 victory, Dobie remarked, "Happy? What's going to happen to us next week?" If one of his players executed a great play, Dobie would emphasize the negative. In 1920, Cornell defensive end Dave Munns made a game-saving tackle against

Colgate by grabbing the ballcarrier's arm and throwing him to the ground. Dobie chastised the player: "If his arm had come off, they'd had six points." One of the few times he looked on the bright side was after his Cornell team was smashed by Dartmouth 62–13. Dobie told sportswriter Grantland Rice that as far as he was concerned, his team had won 13–0. "I don't count those scores made by passing," he explained. "That isn't football." After coaching 14 teams to undefeated seasons, Dobie's 1935 Cornell squad went winless. The dour coach shook his head and said, ""You can't win with Phi Beta Kappas."

2. **DICK TOMEY**

Probably the most bizarre motivational ploy belonged to University of Hawaii coach Dick Tomey. In August, 1985, he had his players walk barefoot over a 12-foot bed of glowing coals. The purpose of the painful exercise was to help players overcome their fears. Discovering that the only thing they had to fear was fear itself—and their opponents—the Rainbow Warriors finished the season with a 4–6–2 record.

3. **ROBERT ZUPPKE**

Legendary Illinois coach Robert Zuppke was born in Berlin in 1879. Using unconventional coaching methods, he led the Fighting Illini to undefeated seasons in 1914, 1915, 1923, and 1927. A great innovator, he introduced the huddle, flea flicker, and screen pass, and he designed a model for an early football helmet. A complex and sometimes contradictory man, Zuppke was a serious student of philosophy and an author of humorous stories. He also raised hogs. George Halas played for Zuppke and learned many of his coaching techniques from him. Zuppke's greatest player, Red Grange, called him "the best psychiatrist I ever met." Oddly, Zuppke tried to dissuade Grange from playing professional football because he thought it should be played for the love of the game and not for money. It was Zuppke who said, "Football is not a contact sport. Dancing is a contact sport. Football is a collision sport."

4. WEEPING WALLY BUTTS

Wally Butts coached the University of Georgia from 1939 to 1960. Known as "Weeping Wally" because of the sob stories he told his players to motivate them, Butts' most memorable moment occurred at halftime of a 1946 game against Furman. Ahead 28–7, Butts was still unhappy with his team's play. In the locker room, Butts kicked a potbellied stove, causing the pipe connecting it to the wall to collapse, filling the room with black soot. Despite the halftime debacle, Georgia went on to a 70–7 win.

5. FIELDING YOST

Fielding Yost coached the University of Michigan from 1901 to 1926. Yost's teams won 196 games and lost only 36. Notorious for his verbosity, Yost was nicknamed "Hurry Up" because he always said it to his players. Grantland Rice told a story about once seeing Yost in an argument with another coach in a hotel lobby. When Rice returned seven hours later, Yost was still lecturing the man. "I couldn't get in one word," the other coach admitted.

6. LARRY JONES

One of the most unusual training methods was practiced by Florida State's coach Larry Jones in 1973. Jones devised a training room that was enclosed by chicken wire. Players were forced to endure brutal one-on-one drills and some left the room battered and bloody. The training regimen was so hard that 28 players quit the team. The demoralized Seminoles lost all 11 games and Jones was fired.

7. FRANK KUSH

Frank Kush coached Arizona State from 1958 to 1979. His Sun Devil teams won 176 games and lost only 54. Although no one could argue with his results, some questioned his methods. One of Kush's controversial training techniques was the infamous "Hamburger Drill." He encircled a player with members of his defensive team and the unfortunate man-in-the-middle had to block each of them one at a time, sometimes until he collapsed. The punishment for a receiver who dropped a pass was a drill in which high passes were thrown at him. When the receiver jumped to catch them, a defensive player would undercut him. Kush was fired in 1979 after a former player, Kevin Rutledge, accused the coach of punching him in the mouth.

8. JOHN HARPO VAUGHT

John Harpo Vaught coached the University of Mississippi from 1947 to 1973. His Ole Miss teams won six Southeastern Conference titles, ten bowl games, and went undefeated four seasons. Vaught insisted that his strict rules be obeyed. Players were not allowed to be married or own a car.

9. GEORGE WOODRUFF

University of Pennsylvania coach George Woodruff won more games in his first ten seasons than any head coach in college football history. From 1892 to 1901, Woodruff's teams won 124 games and lost only 15. Woodruff is credited with inventing the "flying wedge," a V-shaped blocking formation which was almost impossible to penetrate. Despite his success, Woodruff was fired following the 1901 season because Pennsylvania had lost three consecutive years to rival Harvard. Woodruff, a Phi Beta Kappa graduate of Yale, served as acting secretary of the interior in 1907 and was the Pennsylvania attorney general from 1923 to 1927.

10. RICHARD NIXON

The nation's number-one armchair quarterback, Richard Nixon couldn't resist offering plays to the coaches of his favorite teams. As president, he suggested plays to Washington Redskins' coach George Allen. Unfortunately, the plays never seemed to work. Prior to Super Bowl VI, Nixon called Miami Dolphins' coach Don Shula and suggested a surefire pass play to wide receiver Paul Warfield. Every time the play was called, the pass was either incomplete or intercepted. The Dolphins lost to the Dallas Cowboys 24–3. After the Dolphins won the Super Bowl the following year, Shula publicly thanked Nixon for not suggesting any more plays.

SEASONS TO FORGET

Some universities such as Notre Dame and Michigan have long winning traditions in football. The opposite is true for schools such as Northwestern and Columbia. In the pros, the Dallas Cowboys and San Francisco Forty-Niners have become synonymous with winning. On the other hand, the New Orleans Saints and Cincinnati Bengals have histories of futility. The teams in this list just couldn't win.

1. BETHEL HIGH

In 1974, the Bethel High School football team from Brandt, Ohio, was shut out in every game. They lost by the scores of 40–0, 53–0, 92–0, 89–0, 50–0, 56–0, 36–0, 33–0, 46–0, and 49–0. The game in which they lost 89–0 was called three minutes into the second half to spare further embarrassment. The coach of the team, often mentioned as the worst in high school football history, was named Dennis Reck.

2. TAMPA BAY BUCCANEERS

The expansion Tampa Bay Buccaneers lost their first 26 games. The 1976 team lost all 14 games. Their offense was so anemic that the Bucs were shut out a dozen times during their losing streak. Tampa Bay scored only three points in their first six home games. When coach John McKay was asked what he thought of his team's execution, he replied, "I'm in favor of it." The streak finally ended on December 11, 1977, when Tampa Bay upset the New Orleans Saints 33–14. The Saints' fans were so ashamed that many wore paper bags over their heads to conceal their identities.

3. CINCINNATI REDS

If there's any team in NFL history that was worse than the 1976 Tampa Bay Buccaneers, it was the 1934 Cincinnati Reds. The Reds lost all eight of the games and were outscored 243–10 for the season. On November 6, 1934, they lost 64–0 to the Philadelphia Eagles, the worst regular-season loss in league history. Following the loss the team disbanded. The last three games were played by a semi-pro team called The St. Louis Gunners.

4. CARD-PITT

One of the truly dreadful teams in NFL history, the 1944 Card-Pitt squad lost all ten of its games. For that season only, the Chicago Cardinals and Pittsburgh Steelers teams were combined as a cost-cutting measure. The team was so bad that it was nicknamed the "Carpets" because every team walked all over them.

5. NORTHWESTERN

From September 22, 1979, to September 18, 1982, the Northwestern Wildcats lost 32 games in a row. During the period from 1976 to 1982, the Wildcats won three games and lost 65. The 1981 team was so bad that they were outscored by an average of 40 points per game. After a 61–14 drubbing by Michigan State, Northwestern students tore down the goal posts and carried them through the streets of Evanston, Illinois, chanting, "We're the worst!" The streak finally ended in 1982 when Northwestern defeated Northern Illinois 31–6.

6. MACALESTER COLLEGE

Macalester College, located in St. Paul, Minnesota, lost 50 consecutive games from 1974 to 1980. The lowest point came in 1977 when they lost to Concordia Moorhead by the score of 97–6. On September 6, 1980, the losing streak came to an end when the Scots defeated Mount Scenario College of Wisconsin 17–14.

7. ST. PAUL'S POLY

St. Paul's Poly, a college in Virginia, lost 41 games in a row between 1947 and 1953. During one stretch, they were outscored 890 points to zero.

8. PHILADELPHIA EAGLES

The 1936 Philadelphia Eagles had one of the worst offenses in pro football history. The Eagles won only one of 12 games and scored only 51 points a season. Eagles' quarterbacks completed only 31 passes all year and threw 35 interceptions.

9. DAYTON TRIANGLES

The 1928 Dayton Triangles lost all seven games and were outscored 131 points to nine. To prove it was no fluke, the 1929 Triangles lost all six games and scored only seven points. The team wisely disbanded after the 1929 NFL season.

10. ROCHESTER JEFFERSONS

The Rochester Jeffersons were one of the early NFL franchises. During their final four seasons, 1922–1925, Rochester did not win a game. Over that span the Jeffersons lost 21 games while scoring only 52 points, an average of only 13 points per year.

RUNNING UP THE SCORE

In football, it's generally considered bad sportsmanship to run up the score. This unwritten rule didn't stop these teams from being involved in some of football's biggest blowouts.

1. GEORGIA TECH

The biggest blowout in college football history occurred on October 7, 1916, when mighty Georgia Tech met tiny Cumberland College. The Yellow Jackets, coached by famed John Heisman, were one of the best teams in the country while Cumberland College, coached by a law student named Butch McQueen, were barely able to field a team. To make matters worse, several Cumberland players got lost and missed the game. One player, Gentry Dugat, had to have the rules explained to him. It was a rout from the opening kickoff. Georgia Tech led 63–0 at the end of the first quarter, and by halftime the score had ballooned to 126–0. Even though the second half was shortened by fifteen minutes, the massacre continued. Cumberland fumbled nine times. After he fumbled, a player yelled to a teammate to recover it. The terrified player replied, "You pick it up. You dropped it." In the fourth quarter, Heisman discovered a Cumberland player on the bench, hiding under a blanket. When it was finally over, Georgia Tech had overwhelmed Cumberland by the score of 222–0. Without attempting a pass, Georgia Tech had scored 32 touchdowns and gained 1,179 total yards. They scored on 19 of 29 rushes and averaged more than 17 yards per rushing attempt. Incredibly, the Cumberland players celebrated on the train ride back to their Tennessee campus. After all, none of the players had been killed.

2. KING COLLEGE

On October 21, 1922, King College defeated Lenoir 206–0 in a game played in Bristol, Tennessee.

3. PORTLAND STATE

Led by quarterback Neil Lomax's eight touchdown passes, Portland State clobbered Delaware State 105–0 in a game played on November 8, 1980. The 105 points were the most ever scored by a Division I-AA college.

4. HOUSTON

In a flagrant example of running up the score, Houston humiliated Tulsa 100–6 in a game played at the Astrodome on November 23, 1968. Eleven different players scored touchdowns, including a 27-yard score by future country music star Larry Gatlin. Running back Paul Gipson rushed for 282 yards as the Cougars rolled up 762 yards in total offense. Eager to avenge a 22–13 loss to Tulsa the previous year, Houston scored 49 points in the fourth quarter.

5. WEST VIRGINIA

Another of the biggest routs in college football history, West Virginia defeated Marshall 92–6 on November 6, 1915.

Marshall's only touchdown came when Blondie Taylor climbed on the shoulders of end Dayton Carter and caught a touchdown lob. West Virginia coach Charles Metzger protested the play in vain.

6. MISSISSIPPI STATE

Superstar wide receiver Jerry Rice caught 17 passes for 294 yards as Mississippi State shut out Kentucky State 86–0 on September 1, 1984. Quarterback Willie Totten passed for 536 yards.

7. CHICAGO BEARS

No one could have anticipated that the 1940 championship game between the Chicago Bears and the Washington Redskins would be the most lopsided game in NFL history. Three weeks before the championship game, the Redskins had defeated the Bears 7–3. After that game, Washington owner George Preston Marshall called the Bears a bunch of crybabies. Motivated by the comments, Chicago destroyed Washington by the score of 73–0. The Bears scored so many touchdowns that they had to pass on their last two points after touchdowns because they'd run out of footballs.

8. ALABAMA

The biggest blowout in college bowl history took place in the 1953 Orange Bowl when Alabama pounded Syracuse 61–6.

9. MICHIGAN

The first Rose Bowl, a 1902 contest between Michigan and Stanford, was almost the last. Michigan entered the game as a prohibitive favorite. During the season the undefeated Wolverines had outscored their opponents 555–0. They led

Stanford 49–0 in the fourth quarter when they agreed to stop the slaughter with eight minutes remaining. The game was such a debacle that the Rose Bowl was discontinued until 1916.

10. OAKLAND

The Oakland Raiders defeated the Denver Broncos 51–0 in an AFL game played on September 10, 1967. The Raiders' defense was so dominant that the Broncos had a minus-five-yards total offense.

UNUSUAL BOWL GAMES

During the holiday season, the best college football teams are matched in numerous bowl games. While most of us have watched the Rose Bowl or Orange Bowl on television, a number of less successful bowls have been staged over the years. Some of the bowls which have come and gone include the Cigar Bowl, Ice Bowl, Vulcan Bowl, Glass Bowl, Fruit Bowl, Oleander Bowl, Botany Bowl, Paper Bowl, Spindletop Bowl, Bean Bowl, Bamboo Bowl, Bacardi Bowl, Boot Hill Bowl, Cattle Bowl, Space City Bowl, Cement Bowl, Optimist Bowl, Shrimp Bowl, Yam Bowl, Pretzel Bowl, and Pythian Bowl.

1. IODINE BOWL

The Iodine Bowl was played in Charleston, South Carolina, from 1949 to 1953. Allen College won the bowl three times during its brief existence.

2. POINSETTIA BOWL

The inaugural Poinsettia Bowl was played on December 20, 1952, at San Diego's Balboa Stadium. The game between the San Diego Naval Training Center and the Bolling Air

Force Base didn't exactly generate fan interest. When it rained heavily on the day of the game, hundreds of reluctant sailors were rounded up to sit through the downpour so that the stands would not appear empty during the nationally televised game. Bolling won by the score of 35–14.

3. REFRIGERATOR BOWL

Evansville, Indiana, hosted the Refrigerator Bowl, which lasted from 1948 until 1956. The local university, Evansville, won the first two Refrigerator Bowls.

4. KICKAPOO BOWL

The one and only Kickapoo Bowl was played on December 5, 1947, in Wichita Falls, Texas. Midwestern State defeated Central Arkansas 39–20 before a crowd of 5,000 fans.

5. FISH BOWL

There were actually two Fish Bowls played in two different cities in one year. In November, 1948, Southwestern defeated Corpus Christi 7–0 in the Fish Bowl played in Corpus Christi, Texas. A month later, in Norfolk, Virginia, Hampton edged Central State 20–19 in a second Fish Bowl.

6. BOY'S RANCH BOWL

Missouri Valley defeated McMurry 20–13 in the only Boy's Ranch Bowl, played in Abilene, Texas on December 13, 1947.

7. TURKEY BOWL

The Turkey Bowl was played in Indiana on November 28, 1946. Evansville defeated Northern Illinois by the score of 19–7. The game was such a turkey that the bowl was discontinued.

8. SPAGHETTI BOWL

Spaghetti Bowls, featuring armed services teams, were played in Florence, Italy, in 1945 and 1953. Army squads defeated Air Force teams in both games.

9. SALAD BOWL

The Salad Bowl was played in Phoenix, Arizona, from 1948 to 1954. Winners included Nevada, Xavier, Miami of Ohio, and Houston.

10. CHIGGER BOWL

Dutch Guiana may seem like an unlikely venue for a football game, but it was the site of the Chigger Bowl on January 1, 1945. The Army Air Base Bonecrushers outlasted the Army Airway Rams 6–0.

STEAMROLLERS AND ESKIMOS

The American Professional Football Association, which later became the NFL, was founded on September 17, 1920, in Canton, Ohio. The meeting took place in a Hupmobile showroom. The league consisted of teams from five states. Owners could purchase a franchise for one hundred dollars. Today, NFL franchises are worth hundreds of millions of dollars. Here's a lineup of some of professional football's least likely franchises.

1. OORANG INDIANS

Unquestionably, the most unusual franchise in NFL history was the Oorang Indians. The team was the brainchild of Walter Lingo, owner of the Oorang Dog Kennels in LaRue, a small town in Ohio. Lingo, inspired by the brilliant play of Jim Thorpe, decided to have a team comprised entirely of Native Americans. The roster included Big Bear, Dick Deer Slayer, Eagle Feather, Long Time Sleep, Joe Little Twig, Ted Lone Wolf, Red Fang, David Running Deer, War Eagle, White Cloud, Deadeye, Xavier Downwind, Laughing Gas, Gray Horse, Baptiste Thunder, Tomahawk Arrowhead, and Woodchuck Wolmas. The team, whose principal purpose was to promote the owner's kennels, folded in 1923 in its second year of existence.

2. RACINE CARDINALS

One of the charter members of the NFL, the Racine Cardinals were named after a street in Chicago. In the early years, the team played at Normal Field located on the corner of Racine Avenue and Normal Boulevard. The team changed its name to the Chicago Cardinals in 1922 when a team from Racine, Wisconsin, joined the league. The Cardinals later moved to St. Louis and are now located in Phoenix.

3. DULUTH ESKIMOS

The Duluth Eskimos were an NFL franchise from 1923 until 1927. The Eskimos have the distinction of being the only team to wear an igloo insignia on its jerseys. For a few years the team was owned on a cooperative basis, with each player owning a share. In 1926, Ole Haugsrud and Dewey Scanlon purchased the team for one dollar. With only 13 players in uniform, owner Ole Haugsrud occasionally suited up for games. In a game against the St. Louis Gunners, Haugsrud sent himself in to punt. His teammates refused to block, and he was flattened by the St. Louis defense.

4. POTTSVILLE MAROONS

During their brief tenure in the NFL, the Pottsville (Pennsylvania) Maroons were one of the league's most successful teams. In 1925, their first season, they compiled a 10–2 record. When they defeated the Chicago Cardinals 21–7 late in the season, they declared themselves the league champions. Capitalizing on their notoriety, they agreed to play a team of Notre Dame All-Stars, despite threats from the league president Joe Carr, who declared the exhibition game was against league rules. As a result, the Maroons were expelled from the league, and the Cardinals were declared champions. Fans tried to soothe the players' disappointment by presenting them with a life-size trophy of a football made entirely of anthracite coal. Pottsville was reinstated the following year and remained in the league until 1929.

5. PROVIDENCE STEAM ROLLER

The Providence Steam Roller played in a stadium that had been built for bicycle racing. The Cyclodrome had a banked wooden track that encompassed the playing field. The strange configuration included one end zone that was only five yards deep. Despite the odd stadium and team name, the Steam Roller compiled a 41–32–11 record in the NFL from 1925 to 1931.

6. COLUMBUS PANHANDLES

Most of the players on the Columbus Panhandles were employees of the Panhandle Division of the Pennsylvania Railroad. Because they had free rail passes and no practice field of their own, the team played most of its games on the road. In a December 4, 1921, game against Louisville, five brothers from the Nesser family (Frank, Fred, John, Phil, and Ted) played for Columbus. In addition, Ted's son Charles also played, marking the only time in NFL history that a father and son played in the same game. When the team disbanded in 1926, its lifetime record was 13 wins, 45 losses, and three ties.

7. DECATUR STALEYS

The Decatur Staleys were one of the original NFL teams. They were the creation of A.E. Staley, owner of the Staley

Starch Works in Decatur, Illinois. When his starch business took a downturn, Staley turned the team over to player-coach George Halas. By 1922, the team had moved to Chicago and changed its name to the Bears.

8. FRANKFORD YELLOW JACKETS

The Frankford Yellow Jackets were named for a Philadelphia suburb. Due to the Pennsylvania blue laws in force at the time, the Yellow Jackets were not permitted to play home games on Sunday. Instead, they played at home on Saturday and occasionally took a train to play on the road the following day. As a result, they usually played more games than any other team in the league. Frankford won the 1926 NFL championship and remained in the league until 1931.

9. RACINE LEGION

The Racine Legion were sponsored by American Legion Post 76 of Racine, Wisconsin. In 1923, the Legion Post organized a fund-raising dinner to bail out the financially strapped team. The Legion remained in the league until 1926.

10. TONAWANDA KARDEX

The dubious distinction of being the shortest-lived NFL franchise belongs to the Tonawanda Kardex. The New York team played one road game in 1921, a 45–0 loss to the Rochester Jeffersons, and then folded.

BELIEVE IT OR NOTS

The following entries may be hard to believe, but they're all true.

1. WYLLYS TERRY

In a November 5, 1884, game against Wesleyan, Yale's Wyllys Terry ran 109 yards for a touchdown. The record was possible because the fields measured 110 yards at the time.

2. AL NESSER

Al Nesser, a lineman for the 1926 New York Giants, played an entire game dressed in a bathing suit.

3. UNIVERSITY OF THE SOUTH

On November 14, 1899, the University of the South defeated Mississippi State 12–0. What made the win remarkable was that it was their fifth victory in six days. Despite having an enrollment of less than 100 and a football team with only 12 players, the University of the South defeated Texas, Texas A&M, Tulane, Louisiana State, and Mississippi State in succession.

4. STANFORD MARCHING BAND

You never know what to expect when you're being entertained at halftime by the Stanford Marching Band. They excel at mocking their opponents and have had shows dedicated to everything from condoms to the kidnapping of Patty Hearst. At the end of one show, the band members dropped their pants and mooned the crowd.

5. COLUMBIA MARCHING BAND

If any band can rival Stanford for outrageous behavior then it has to be Columbia. The Ivy League school takes pride in educating its audience. In 1967, at halftime in a game against Yale, the band marched in formations depicting various birth control methods. Another time, in a game with Harvard, the band mocked a proposed constitutional amendment by simulating a flag burning while playing the Doors' "Light My Fire."

6. JERRY GLANVILLE

Outspoken Jerry Glanville coached the Houston Oilers from 1985 to 1989 and the Atlanta Falcons from 1990 to 1993. Glanville had the odd habit of leaving tickets at the will-call window for deceased entertainers. Among those he left tickets for were Elvis Presley, James Dean, and Buddy Holly.

7. ALVIN WISTERT

Alvin Wistert, a tackle for the University of Michigan, was named to the 1948 All-American team. What makes his selection noteworthy is that Wistert was 33 years old. He got a late start in college after serving in the military.

Jon SooHoo

Jerry Glanville

Eccentric head coach Jerry Glanville used to leave tickets for Elvis Presley and other deceased entertainers at the stadium's will-call window.

8. COLGATE

Colgate had a dream season in 1932. The Red Raiders won all nine of their games and outscored the opposition 264 points to zero. Incredibly, they were passed over for bowl consideration.

9. HUNCHY HOERNSCHEMEYER

Halfback Bob "Hunchy" Hoernschemeyer played for the Detroit Lions from 1950 to 1955. During his NFL career, he completed 11 passes. Remarkably, ten of the 11 completions were for touchdowns.

10. SWEDE OBERLANDER

Swede Oberlander was an All-American quarterback with Dartmouth in 1924. He had a strange timing technique for his deep passes. Oberlander would drop back to pass and recite in his mind, "Ten thousand Swedes jumped out of the weeds at the Battle of Copenhagen." If, at this point, he had not already been flattened by the pass rush, he would release the ball.

STRANGE PLAYS

If you think that you've seen everything that can happen on a football field, think again.

1. **ED COOK**

Oklahoma defeated Oklahoma A&M 75–0 on November 6, 1904, but the lopsided score is not why the contest is still remembered. The game, played in South Guthrie, Oklahoma, featured one of the strangest touchdowns on record. It happened in the first quarter as A&M punter B. O. Callahan punted from his end zone. A strong gust of wind blew his punt into Cottonwood Creek, which flowed next to the field. Under the rules of the day, the ball was still in play. Players from both teams dove into the icy water. Oklahoma's Ed Cook, the best swimmer in the group, got to the ball first and swam ten yards for a touchdown.

2. **RED WILSON**

Another bizarre punting incident occurred in a 1904 game between Georgia and Georgia Tech, played in Atlanta's Piedmont Park. Georgia punter Arthur Sullivan kicked from his own end zone. His punt struck the crossbar of the goalpost and bounced over a 16-foot fence behind him. The referee signaled that the ball was still in play. In a mad scramble, players climbed the wall and frantically searched for the football in the bushes. Spectators had no idea what had happened until Georgia Tech's Red Wilson climbed the wall and held up the ball. Wilson was credited with a touchdown as Georgia Tech defeated Georgia 23–6.

3. CHARLIE GOGOLAK

Cornell devised an ingenious way to defend a field goal in an October 9, 1965, game against Princeton. The Tigers' star kicker, Charlie Gogolak, was about to attempt an easy 19-yard field goal when Cornell defensive backs Dave Witwer and Jim Docherty climbed onto the shoulders of linemen Harry Garman and Reeve Vannemann. Although they didn't block the kick, they distracted Gogolak enough that he missed the field goal. Unfortunately for Cornell, an offside penalty negated the play and Princeton went on to score a touchdown in a 36–27 win.

4. SNOOKS DOWD

Lehigh halfback Raymond "Snooks" Dowd ran twice as far as he needed to run in a 1918 game against Lafayette. Dowd began the play by running 15 yards the wrong way into his own end zone. Dowd then ran around the goal post and raced the length of the field for a touchdown. It was estimated that he ran more than 200 yards on the play.

5. KEVIN MOEN

One of the most improbable finishes in college football history took place on November 20, 1982, in a game between

Stanford and California. Stanford led 20–19 with four seconds remaining as California's Kevin Moen fielded a punt at his own 43-yard line. Through a series of five laterals, California moved the ball toward the Stanford goal line. Thinking the game was over, the Stanford band began marching onto the field. Moen, who once again had the ball, used the musicians for interference. As he crossed the goal line with the winning touchdown, Moen knocked over trombone player Gary Tyrrell.

6. JOHN REAVES

Florida players literally laid down in order to give quarterback John Reaves a chance to break a passing record in a November 27, 1971, game against Miami. Late in the game, Florida led comfortably by the score of 45–7. Miami had the ball at the Gators' seven-yard line. When the Florida defenders intentionally fell to the ground, Miami quarterback John Hornibrook was able to run uncontested into the end zone. Given one more possession, John Reaves was able to break Jim Plunkett's record for career passing yards.

7. BULL DOEHRING

Halfback John "Bull" Doehring played with the Chicago Bears in the early 1930s. End Luke Johnsos remembered a play in which Doehring took a lateral while Johnsos raced downfield on a deep pass route. With defenders swarming all over Doehring, Johnsos assumed he would be tackled. He was so amazed that Doehring was able to throw a pass that he dropped it even though it hit him right in the hands. Somehow Doehring had thrown the ball 40 yards behind his back.

8. R.C. OWENS

One of the great leapers in professional football, San Francisco Forty-Niners end R.C. Owens caught the first "Alley Oop" passes from Y.A. Tittle in 1957. His jumping ability was so exceptional that he once blocked a 40-yard field goal attempt by Baltimore's Bob Khayat as the ball was about to go over the crossbar.

9. LEO DICK

Indiana was literally blown away in a game against Iowa on November 8, 1913. Hoosier punter Clair Scott was forced to punt from his own end zone into a 50-mile-per-hour wind. Scott's punt got caught in the wind and began blowing back toward him. Iowa's punt returner, Leo Dick, ran 25 yards forward to catch the ball in the end zone for a windblown touchdown.

10. BOBBY MOORE

St. Louis Cardinals' wide receiver Bobby Moore caught a 98-yard pass in a 1972 game against the Los Angeles Rams and didn't even score a touchdown. The Cardinals were at their own one-yard line when quarterback Jim Hart threw a long pass to Moore, who caught the ball at the 40-yard line and ran toward the end zone. He was dragged down at the one-yard line by Rams' defender Al Clark. St. Louis scored on the next play and won the game 24–14.

THE STRANGEST GAMES EVER PLAYED

Anyone who saw one of these games would have a hard time forgetting it.

1. T.L. BAYNE

Coach T.L. Bayne was preparing his Louisiana State team for a game against Tulane in 1893 when he learned that the opposing team was without a coach for the game. Bayne agreed to coach both LSU and Tulane that day. He soon discovered that he was also responsible for ticket sales, building the goal posts, and refereeing the game. Louisiana State won, making Bayne both the winning and losing coach. For his efforts he was given a green umbrella.

2. THE 1932 NFL TITLE GAME

When an extreme cold spell in Chicago threatened the 1932 NFL Championship Game, the teams decided to play indoors at the Chicago Stadium rather than postpone the game. The field was only 80 yards long and had a dirt surface that had just been used by a circus and still smelled like animals. The Chicago Bears defeated the Portsmouth Spartans 9–0.

3. ARAB BOWL

During World War II, several bowl games were played overseas by armed services personnel. On New Years' Day, 1942, the "Arab Bowl" was played in Oran, North Africa, between teams of Army and Navy all stars. Army won the game 10–7. During halftime, spectators were entertained by camel races featuring WACS and Red Cross nurses as jockeys.

4. GROVER CLEVELAND

Navy defeated Army 6–4 in a hard-fought game in 1893. The rivalry between the armed services was so intense that a brigadier general punched a heckling rear admiral. Reportedly, the two subsequently fought a duel, but both shooters missed their marks. President Grover Cleveland, in order to protect his military leaders, suspended the annual football game between Army and Navy for six years.

5. 1942 ROSE BOWL

The Rose Bowl is an annual tradition in Pasadena, California, but it was held on the East Coast in 1942. Fearful of a potential Japanese air attack, officials agreed to play the game in Durham, North Carolina, where the Duke campus was located. Despite the home-field advantage, Duke lost to Oregon 20–16.

6. TOURNAMENT OF ROSES

From 1903 to 1915, the Rose Bowl contests could be called the strangest games never played. Instead of football games, Tournament of Roses' officials annually staged a number of events including chariot races, ostrich races, polo, rodeo events, and tent pegging. The football game was resumed in 1916.

7. 1942 COTTON BOWL

In one of the most improbable victories in bowl history, Alabama defeated Texas A&M 29–21, despite making only one first down. The key to victory for the Crimson Tide was seven interceptions and five fumble recoveries.

8. CONNIE MACK

On November 26, 1902, the Philadelphia A's, coached by Connie Mack, defeated the Pittsburgh Pros 12–6 to claim the United States Football Championship. Two Hall of Fame baseball pitchers played in the game—Rube Waddell for Philadelphia and Christy Mathewson for Pittsburgh.

9. REDSKINS - GIANTS

In the highest-scoring game in NFL history, the Washington Redskins defeated the New York Giants 72–41 on November 27, 1966. With seven seconds remaining in the game, Redskins' coach Otto Graham sent kicker Charlie Gogolak out to attempt a 29-yard field goal. While it may not have been good sportsmanship, the meaningless field goal did break the record for the most points scored by one team in a regular-season game. The old mark was 70 by the Los Angeles Rams.

10. LIONS - CARDINALS

The September 15, 1940, game between the Detroit Lions and Chicago Cardinals was noteworthy for several reasons.

The game was held in a neutral site—Buffalo, New York—because of small crowds in Chicago. Played in a thunderstorm, the contest ended in a scoreless tie. Due to the terrible weather conditions, the two teams combined for only 30 yards in offense, an NFL record for futility.

NOT FIT FOR MAN NOR BEAST

As a winter sport, football has seen its share of inclement weather. The 1948 NFL Championship Game between the Philadelphia Eagles and the Chicago Cardinals was held in a blinding blizzard. Green Bay and Carolina played the 1997 NFC title game with a wind-chill factor of 25 degrees below zero.

1. THE ICE BOWL

The 1967 NFL Championship Game between the Green Bay Packers and the Dallas Cowboys remains one of the greatest contests in pro football history. With a game-time temperature of 13 degrees below zero and a wind-chill factor of −46 degrees, it's amazing that the game was played at all. More than 50,000 fans braved the cold in Green Bay's Lambeau Field. Packers' quarterback Bart Starr scored the winning touchdown with 13 seconds remaining to give Green Bay a 21–17 victory.

2. THE SNOW BOWL

Although they didn't complete a pass or make a first down, the Michigan Wolverines defeated the Ohio State Buckeyes

9–3 in a November 25, 1950, game which has come to be known as the "Snow Bowl." Played in blizzard conditions, the teams combined for only 68 yards in total offense. There were 45 punts in the game. Michigan managed to win by blocking four Ohio State punts.

3. BENGALS – CHARGERS

The 1981 AFC Championship Game between the Cincinnati Bengals and San Diego Chargers rivaled the Ice Bowl for the worst conditions in NFL history. The wind-chill factor in Cincinnati was 59 degrees below zero. Bengals' quarterback Ken Anderson threw two touchdown passes as Cincinnati defeated San Diego 27–7.

4. THE LAST COLLEGE ALL-STAR GAME

For 43 years the College All-Star Game matched a team of outstanding college players against the defending NFL champions. That tradition ended on July 23, 1976. The Pittsburgh Steelers were leading the College All-Stars 24–0 in the third quarter when a severe thunderstorm roared through Chicago. The game was halted due to torrential rain, high winds, and dangerous lightning. Not only was the game not resumed, but the annual All-Star Game was cancelled.

5. NORTHWESTERN – MICHIGAN

The Windy City lived up to its name in a 1925 matchup of Northwestern and Michigan. The teams endured rain, sleet, and 55-mile-per-hour winds. Northwestern won 3–2 in a game in which only one pass was completed and one first down was made.

6. GEORGE WOODRUFF

Georgia quarterback George "Kid" Woodruff took advantage of a dense fog to throw a touchdown pass in a game against Sewanee on November 5, 1910. The fog hovered over the Tennessee field, making it almost impossible to see for more than a few yards. Georgia was trailing 15–6 in the fourth quarter when Woodruff faded back to pass from the Sewanee 30-yard line. Woodruff took off his helmet and threw it down the left sidelines. Defenders, thinking it was the ball, ran to that area. Woodruff then threw a pass down the right sidelines to Bob McWhorter for an easy touchdown.

7. THE FOG BOWL

The December 31, 1988, playoff game in Chicago between the Chicago Bears and Philadelphia Eagles is known as the "Fog Bowl." The visibility was so bad that television viewers had no idea of what was happening in the game. The Bears prevailed by the score of 20–12.

8. WASHINGTON STATE – SAN JOSE STATE

The weather was so cold at the November 12, 1955, game between Washington State and San Jose State that only one fan paid admission, the smallest crowd in college football history.

9. FLORIDA STATE – WICHITA STATE

Florida State defeated Wichita State 24–0 in a game played in a downpour at Tallahassee on September 20, 1969. Five inches of rain fell during the game, making the ball so slippery that the teams fumbled a record 27 times.

10. **TEXAS TECH – CENTENARY**

Neither team wanted the football in a November 11, 1939, game between Texas Tech and Centenary. A rainstorm in Shreveport, Louisiana, turned the game into a punting contest. The two teams punted a total of 77 times, 33 on first down. The game ended in a 0–0 tie.

WHISTLE BLOWERS

As with other team sports, referees in football have a great deal of impact on the outcome of a game. Plays can be cancelled by penalties, and touchdowns can be called back. In these situations, the officials made the call.

1. RED FRIESELL

Cornell entered its November 16, 1940, game against Dartmouth with an 18-game winning streak. Trailing 3–0, halfback Bill Murphy caught a touchdown pass with three seconds remaining for an apparent 7–3 victory. Only after viewing game films did Cornell coach Carl Snavely realize that his team had been given an extra down. Referee Red Friesell had lost count. Snavely graciously conceded the game to Dartmouth. The conference commissioner sent a telegram to Friesell that read: "Don't let it get you down, down, down, down, down."

2. CIGAR BOWL

On December 30, 1912, the University of Florida football team traveled to Havana to play the Cuban Athletic Club.

The Cigar Bowl's purpose was to promote harmonious relations between Cuba and the U.S. The referee for the game was a former coach of the Cuban team. The Americans discovered quickly that all the calls were going the Cubans' way. The referee called back two Florida touchdowns because of nonexistent penalties. When Florida coach G.E. Pyle protested a 15-yard penalty, the referee offered to cut it to five yards. Outraged, Pyle pulled his players off the field and forfeited the game. Pyle was arrested and fled the country with his team once he was released.

3. BALDY ZABEL

Referee Baldy Zabel single-handedly helped the Beloit Professionals defeat the Green Bay Packers 6–0 in a game played on November 24, 1919. Zabel nullified two Packers' touchdowns with penalties and added five seconds on the clock at the end of the first half so Beloit could score the game's only touchdown. Zabel permitted fans to come onto the field to disrupt Packers' pass patterns and even let one fan trip a Green Bay player who was running down the sidelines on his way to a certain touchdown.

4. TOMMY WHELAN

The Baltimore Colts played host to the Buffalo Bills for the Eastern Division title of the All-American Football Conference on December 12, 1948. The Colts led 17–14 in the fourth quarter when Bills' halfback Chet Mutryn caught a short pass, took a few steps, and fumbled the ball, which Baltimore recovered. Baltimore fans were incensed when head linesman Tommy Whelan ruled it an incomplete pass. The crowd began to riot when Buffalo went on to score the winning touchdown. After the game, several hundred fans poured onto the field. Whelan was knocked to the ground and kicked unmercifully. Players came to the official's aid and pulled him from the grasp of the mob. Whelan was then smuggled out of the stadium as fans threw bottles onto the field and set fires in the seats.

5. ARMEN TERZIAN

The Dallas Cowboys trailed the Minnesota Vikings 14–10 with 32 seconds left in a 1975 playoff game at Metropolitan Stadium in Bloomington, Minnesota. With the ball at midfield, Dallas quarterback Roger Staubach threw a long pass to Drew Pearson, who was streaking toward the end zone. Pearson caught the ball between two defenders for the winning touchdown. The play became known as the "Hail Mary" pass. One fan, who thought offensive pass interference should have been called, threw a whiskey bottle which struck field judge Armen Terzian in the head. Terzian was knocked unconscious but not seriously injured.

6. BILL QUINBY

Denver fans showed little sympathy for a fallen official in a November 11, 1985, game against San Francisco. Side judge Bill Quinby lay on the ground after colliding with a player. Fans pelted Quinby with snowballs while trainers attempted to administer medical aid. The Broncos won the game 17–16.

7. NORM SCHACHTER

In a December 8, 1968, game between Los Angeles and Chicago, an official's mistake cost the Rams a chance at victory. Trailing 17–16, Los Angeles was threatening to score when the officials shortchanged them. The Rams were given only three downs when the officials incorrectly charged them a down in addition to loss of down on a holding penalty. As a result of their mistake, referee Norm Schachter and his crew were suspended for the remainder of the season.

8. PAT HAGGERTY

Referee Pat Haggerty was so star-struck by the presence of actress Elizabeth Taylor that he muffed a simple opening coin toss in a September 24, 1989, game between Washington and Dallas. Taylor was at the game as guest of Dallas Cowboys' owner Jerry Jones. Haggerty invited Taylor to call heads or tails before being reminded that the captains of the visiting team make the call. The Redskins won the second coin toss and the game, 30–7.

9. BILL HALLORAN

The Washington Redskins were trailing the New York Giants 9–7 in the waning seconds of the 1939 Eastern Division title game when the Washington kicker attempted a field goal from the 11-yard line. Everyone on the field, including the Giants, thought the kick was good—everyone except referee Bill Halloran. His call was so disputed that Halloran was banned from the game.

10. DON CHANDLER

Baltimore Colts fans will never forgive officials for crediting Green Bay with a field goal in the 1965 Western Division playoff game. The Colts led 10–7 in the fourth quarter when Green Bay's Don Chandler attempted a 22-yard field goal. Many believed the kick was wide, but it was called good. The Packers won the game 13–10 in overtime on another Chandler field goal.

FOOTBALL'S MOST EMBARRASSING MOMENTS

Football can be a humiliating game. If you make a mistake, it's seen by thousands of fans and sometimes millions of television viewers. These players could run, but they had nowhere to hide.

1. Y.A. TITTLE

Y.A. Tittle is best remembered as a Hall of Fame quarterback, but his most embarrassing moment came as a Louisiana State cornerback. Tittle was on defense in a November 1, 1947, game against Mississippi when he intercepted a pass thrown by Charlie Conerly. The intended receiver, Barney Poole, grabbed Tittle by the belt and tried to pull him down. Tittle's belt broke, and he felt his pants begin to drop. He ran down the field, holding the ball in one hand and holding up his pants with the other. Despite his efforts, his pants slipped lower and lower until they were around his ankles. Tittle was tackled at his own 38-yard line. Besides losing his pants, Tittle's team also lost the game 20–18.

2. BILL CHIPLEY

Washington and Lee defensive end Bill Chipley's mistake actually resulted in a penalty on the opposing team in a game against West Virginia on October 12, 1946. Chipley, dazed by a block, stumbled into the wrong huddle. The West Virginia players were so confused by Chipley being in their huddle that they were called for a delay of game penalty, which stalled their drive. Nevertheless, West Virginia won the game 6–0.

3. WORLD BOWL I

The World Bowl was supposed to be the climax of the inaugural World Football League season. The December 5, 1974, game pitted the Birmingham Americans against the Florida Blazers. The league was so financially strapped that both teams hadn't been paid in weeks. Birmingham won the World Bowl 22–21, but the team's celebration was short-lived. During the clubhouse celebration, creditors seized their uniforms.

4. REX KEELING

Cincinnati Bengals' punter Rex Keeling's debut was so dismal that he was fired at halftime. Keeling had been selling cars in Alabama when he received a call from the Bengals. Their regular punter, Dale Livingston, had been called for military duty, and they wanted Keeling to fill in during their December 1, 1968, game against the Boston Patriots. Keeling's debut was less than auspicious. In the first half, he had a punt blocked and averaged only 28 yards per kick. At halftime, an irate coach Paul Brown fired Keeling. Brown's son, Mike, wrote Keeling a check for a game's pay, then the punter was told to leave.

5. LEON LETT

Dallas Cowboys' defensive tackle Leon Lett scooped up a fumble late in Super Bowl XXVII against the Denver Broncos. As he rambled toward the goal line, he began to celebrate and held out the ball. Just as Lett was about to cross the goal line, Denver receiver Don Beebe knocked the ball from Lett's hand, and it rolled through the end zone for a touchback. Dallas won the game anyway, 52–17.

6. JOHNNY LATTNER

Notre Dame halfback Johnny Lattner fumbled five times in a 26–14 loss to Purdue on October 18, 1952. Coach Frank Leahy was so mad that he made Lattner carry a football with a handle around campus for a week. Lattner learned his lesson and won the Heisman Trophy the following year.

7. DAVE SMITH

Pittsburgh Steelers' receiver Dave Smith had his most embarrassing moment during a 1971 Monday Night Football game against Kansas City. In the fourth quarter of a 38–16 loss, Smith caught a pass from Terry Bradshaw and was on his way to an apparent touchdown when he lost track of his progress and spiked the ball on the five-yard line. The ball bounced through the end zone for a touchback.

8. BOBBY YANDELL

Mississippi halfback Bobby Yandell made an unbelievalbe error that cost his team a victory against Mississippi State on November 29, 1941. In the second quarter, teammate Ray Poole caught a pass and was running for a touchdown when Yandell inexplicably tackled him at the Bulldogs' 46-yard line. Mississippi lost the game 6–0.

9. JOHN ELWAY

Denver Broncos' quarterback John Elway had many memorable moments and at least one he'd rather forget. During the fourth quarter of a November 27, 1983, game against San Diego, Elway had his team in a hurry-up offense. The rookie mistakenly lined up behind left guard Tom Glassic instead of center Billy Bryan. Elway became aware of his error only when the center yelled for him to move over. Denver lost the game 31–7.

10. SEAN LANDETA

On January 5, 1986, the New York Giants met the Chicago Bears in a playoff game in Chicago. In the first quarter, the Giants' Sean Landeta punted from his own 12-yard line. The ball squibbed off the side of his foot and was picked up by Chicago's Shaun Gayle, who ran it in for a touchdown. Landeta was credited with a minus-seven-yard punt. The Bears defeated the Giants 21–0.

ULTIMATE UPSETS

Relive some of the biggest upsets in football history.

1. CENTRE – HARVARD

No one believed Centre College had a chance when they met mighty Harvard on October 29, 1921. Harvard had won 25 games in a row, including the 1920 Rose Bowl. Centre was a small college in Kentucky with an enrollment of less than 300 students. To everyone's surprise, the Praying Colonels upset Harvard 6–0 on a 32-yard touchdown run by quarterback Bo McMillan. It was Harvard's first intersectional loss in 40 years.

2. SUPER BOWL III

Everyone expected Super Bowl III to be another easy victory for the NFL. National Football League teams had beaten AFL champions by an average of 22 points in the first two Super Bowls. The Baltimore Colts were installed as 18-point favorites over the New York Jets. The Colts had lost only one game all season and had just blown out the Cleveland Browns 34–0 in the NFL championship game. The only person who seemed to believe in the Jets was their cocky quarterback, Joe Namath, who guaranteed a New York victory. Namath and the Jets shocked the world as New York upset Baltimore 16–7.

3. CARNEGIE TECH – NOTRE DAME

A week after Knute Rockne gave his famous "Win one for the Gipper" speech, Notre Dame played Carnegie Tech in what was expected to be a laugher. The game was a laugher, but it was underdog Carnegie Tech that came out on top 27–7. The defeat was the Fighting Irish's first home loss in 23 years.

4. ILLINOIS – MINNESOTA

Illinois was a 40-point underdog in their 1916 game against Minnesota. Illinois coach Robert Zuppke delivered a strange pep talk before the game. He told his players, "I am Louis XIV, and you are my court. After me, the deluge! Today, I want you to have fun. Even if you lose 100 to nothing, have fun." Illinois players took their coach's advice and upset Minnesota 14–9.

5. COLUMBIA – ARMY

Army entered its October 25, 1947, game against Columbia unbeaten and unscored upon. By contrast, Columbia had just suffered a 20-point loss to Pennsylvania. Columbia overcame a 13-point halftime deficit to defeat Army 21–20. The upset snapped the Cadets' 32-game unbeaten streak.

6. COLUMBIA – STANFORD

Columbia was expected to be no match for Stanford in the 1934 Rose Bowl. Stanford outgained Columbia 272 yards to 114, but Columbia still won the game 7–0.

7. NOTRE DAME – OKLAHOMA

Oklahoma carried a 47-game winning streak into their November 16, 1957, game against Notre Dame. The Irish, coming off back-to-back losses to Navy and Michigan State, were installed as 18-point underdogs. Notre Dame's Dick Lynch scored the game's only touchdown on a three-yard run in the fourth quarter as the Fighting Irish ended the Sooners' win streak 7–0.

8. HOLY CROSS – BOSTON COLLEGE

Boston College was undefeated and ranked number one in the country when they played Holy Cross in Fenway Park on November 28, 1942. They had outscored their opponents 249–19 in their eight wins. Holy Cross had a mediocre 4–4–1 record entering the game. Nothing went right for Boston College, and Holy Cross rolled to a 55–12 victory. Boston College players cancelled a victory party that had been planned at Boston's famed night club, the Cocoanut Grove, that evening. Losing the national championship may have been the best thing that ever happened to the team. That night, the Cocoanut Grove caught fire, and 491 people died.

9. SUPER BOWL IV

Despite the AFL's victory in Super Bowl III, the NFL's Minnesota Vikings were a prohibitive favorite over the Kansas City Chiefs in Super Bowl IV. The Vikings, led by their Purple People Eater defense, had a 12-game winning streak during the season, and three times scored more than 50 points. Once again the experts were fooled as the Chiefs easily defeated the Vikings 23–7.

10. SUPER BOWL XXXII

Few gave the Denver Broncos a chance when they met the defending Super Bowl champion Green Bay Packers in Super Bowl XXXII. Denver had lost in all four of its previous Super Bowl appearances while the Packers had won the Super Bowl three times. Denver, a 13-point underdog, won the game 31–24 on a fourth-quarter touchdown run by Terrell Davis.

NOT SO SUPER PERFORMANCES

Not everyone can be a Super Bowl hero. The following players and coaches had less than super performances in the biggest games of their lives.

1. MARV LEVY

Buffalo Bills' coach Marv Levy suffered through four consecutive Super Bowl losses. After a heartbreaking 20–19 defeat to the New York Giants in Super Bowl XXV, Levy's Bills lost to Washington 37–24, Dallas 52–17, and once again to the Cowboys 30–13.

2. BUD GRANT

Another coach with an 0–4 record in the Super Bowl was Minnesota's Bud Grant. His Vikings fell to Kansas City 23–7 in Super Bowl IV. The Miami Dolphins defeated Minnesota 24–7 in Super Bowl VIII. The next year the Vikings lost to the Pittsburgh Steelers 16–6. Grant's final appearance in the Super Bowl resulted in a 32–14 trouncing by the Oakland Raiders.

3. DAN REEVES

Dan Reeves coached four teams to the Super Bowl, and each time his squad was defeated by more than two touchdowns. In Super Bowl XXI, Reeves' Denver Broncos were knocked off by the New York Giants 39–20. The next year, the Washington Redskins blasted the Broncos 42–10. The San Francisco Forty-Niners humiliated Denver 55–10 in Super Bowl XXIV. Nine years later, Reeves led the Atlanta Falcons to the Super Bowl against the team he had once coached, the Denver Broncos. This time, with Reeves on the other sidelines, Denver prevailed, 34–19.

4. JACKIE SMITH

Tight end Jackie Smith had a distinguished career in which he caught 480 passes for nearly 8,000 yards, but unfortunately, he will always be remembered for the one he dropped. In Super Bowl XIII, Smith, wide open in the end zone, dropped a third-quarter pass from Roger Staubach which would have tied the game with Pittsburgh. The dropped pass proved costly as the Dallas Cowboys lost 35–31. It was Smith's last game as a professional.

5. CRAIG MORTON

Quarterback Craig Morton saved his worst days for the Super Bowl. He threw three interceptions as his Dallas Cowboys lost 16–13 to the Baltimore Colts in Super Bowl V. Seven years later, Morton was quarterback of the Denver Broncos in Super Bowl XII against the Dallas Cowboys. Morton completed only four passes and threw four interceptions in a 27–10 loss.

6. FRAN TARKENTON

Minnesota quarterback Fran Tarkenton reached the Super Bowl on three occasions but came away empty each time. In appearances against Miami, Pittsburgh, and Oakland, Tarkenton threw a total of six interceptions, and his teams were outscored 72–27.

7. THURMAN THOMAS

Buffalo running back Thurman Thomas participated in four consecutive Super Bowl losses. Thomas played great in his first Super Bowl, gaining 135 yards in a 20–19 loss to the Giants. In Super Bowl XXVI against Washington, he missed the first possession because he lost his helmet and gained only 13 yards for the game. The next year, in a 52–17 loss to Dallas, Thomas rushed for only 19 yards in 11 carries and had a fumble. Thomas gained 37 yards on 16 carries in Super Bowl XXVIII, a 30–13 loss to the Cowboys.

8. EARL MORRALL

Part of the reason for the Baltimore Colts' shocking defeat against the New York Jets in Super Bowl III was the uninspired play of quarterback Earl Morrall. He completed only six of 17 passes and threw three interceptions in the 16–7 loss. Morrall also didn't see receiver Jimmy Orr wide open in the end zone on a play that could have changed the whole complexion of the game.

9. SCOTT NORWOOD

Buffalo Bills' kicker Scott Norwood was brought in to attempt a 47-yard field goal with four seconds remaining in Super

Bowl XXV and his team trailing the New York Giants 20–19. If he makes the field goal, he's a hero and his team wins the Super Bowl. Instead, Norwood's kick missed to the right and Buffalo went on to lose four straight Super Bowls.

10. **DAVID WOODLEY**

Young quarterback David Woodley led the Miami Dolphins to Super Bowl XVII against the Washington Redskins. Woodley completed only four passes as the Dolphins fell to the Redskins 27–17. The next season Woodley was replaced by rookie sensation Dan Marino.

THEY NEVER WON THE SUPER BOWL

Many of the National Football League's greatest players have never played on a Super Bowl winner. Here are ten football immortals who never got to wear the ring.

1. DAN MARINO

Dan Marino holds almost every NFL quarterback record. He threw 420 touchdowns and passed for more than 60,000 yards in his career. The one accomplishment missing from his resume is a Super Bowl victory. In his only appearance in the big game, Marino and his Miami Dolphins lost to Joe Montana and the San Francisco Forty-Niners 38–16 in Super Bowl XIX.

2. BARRY SANDERS

Detroit Lions running back Barry Sanders retired in 1999 as the second leading rusher in NFL history. Sanders led the league in rushing four times in ten seasons, but never made it to the Super Bowl.

3. DICK BUTKUS

For nine seasons, linebacker Dick Butkus was one of the greatest defensive players of all time. Butkus had the misfortune of playing on weak Chicago Bears teams and never reached the Super Bowl.

4. GALE SAYERS

Running back Gale Sayers suffered the same fate as Dick Butkus—he played for the woeful Bears. On top of that, his career was cut short by knee injuries.

5. FRAN TARKENTON

Quarterback Fran Tarkenton threw 342 touchdown passes during his 18-year NFL career. Three times Tarkenton reached the Super Bowl with the Minnesota Vikings and three times he lost.

6. ANTHONY MUNOZ

Often called the greatest offensive lineman in pro football history, tackle Anthony Munoz starred for the Cincinnati Bengals from 1980 to 1992. Munoz played in two Super Bowls with the Bengals, but both times they lost to the San Francisco Forty-Niners.

7. O.J. SIMPSON

One of the most explosive runners of all time, O.J. Simpson had the misfortune of playing for the weak Buffalo Bills teams of the 1970s. The first man to rush for 2,000 yards in a season never played in the Super Bowl.

8. ERIC DICKERSON

Another 2,000-yard rusher, Eric Dickerson led the NFL in rushing four times between 1983 and 1988. However, like Simpson, Dickerson couldn't run his way into the Super Bowl.

9. DEACON JONES

Defensive end Deacon Jones appeared in eight Pro Bowls during his 14 seasons. Despite playing for several strong Los Angeles Rams teams, Jones never made it to the Super Bowl.

10. EARL CAMPBELL

Earl Campbell topped the league in rushing his first three seasons. Although he led the Houston Oilers to two AFC championship games, Campbell never played in the Super Bowl.

UNLIKELY SUPER HEROES

Super Bowl heroes aren't always future Hall of Famers. Sometimes lesser-known players step into the spotlight on Super Bowl Sunday.

1. MAX MCGEE

One player who definitely rose to the occasion in the Super Bowl was Green Bay Packers' end Max McGee. Nearing the close of his career, McGee caught only four passes during the entire 1966 season. Subbing for an injured Boyd Dowler in Super Bowl I, McGee caught seven passes for 138 yards and two touchdowns in the Packers' 35–10 victory over the Kansas City Chiefs. In Super Bowl II, the final game of his career, McGee caught a 35-yard pass in Green Bay's 33–14 win over the Oakland Raiders. McGee's reception yardage for the entire 1967 season was only 33 yards.

2. TIMMY SMITH

Little-used running back Timmy Smith set a Super Bowl record when he rushed for 204 yards, leading the Washington

Redskins to a 42–10 win over the Denver Broncos in Super Bowl XXII. The rookie had rushed for only 126 yards during the 1987 season.

3. JACK SQUIREK

Los Angeles Raiders linebacker Jack Squirek returned an interception for a touchdown in his team's 38–9 rout of the Washington Redskins in Super Bowl XVIII. In five seasons with the Raiders, Squirek had only one other interception.

4. KENNY KING

Running back Kenny King caught an 80-yard touchdown pass from Jim Plunkett as his Oakland Raiders defeated the Philadelphia Eagles 27–10 in Super Bowl XV. During his seven-year career, King had just one other touchdown reception.

5. DESMOND HOWARD

Considered a disappointment as a professional, former Heisman Trophy winner Desmond Howard redeemed himself with an MVP performance in Super Bowl XXXI. Howard, who had never run back a kickoff for a touchdown as a pro, raced 99 yards for a touchdown as the Green Bay Packers defeated the New England Patriots 35–21. Howard's 244 return yards set a Super Bowl record.

6. ROD MARTIN

The defensive star of Super Bowl XV was Oakland linebacker Rod Martin. He intercepted three passes in the Raiders' 27–10 win over the Philadelphia Eagles. Martin had only two interceptions during the entire 1980 season.

7. LARRY BROWN

The Dallas Cowboys won Super Bowl XXX against the Pittsburgh Steelers, but the Most Valuable Player was neither Troy Aikman nor Emmett Smith. Cornerback Larry Brown won the award after intercepting two passes in the 27–17 victory.

8. JIM O'BRIEN

Rookie place kicker Jim O'Brien faced the ultimate pressure situation in Super Bowl V. Brought in with five seconds remaining in the game, O'Brien kicked a 32-yard field goal to give the Baltimore Colts a 16–13 victory against the Dallas Cowboys.

9. STANFORD JENNINGS

Stanford Jennings had only one kickoff return for a touchdown in his nine-year career. He matched that total with a 93-yard return in Super Bowl XXIII. The touchdown gave the Cincinnati Bengals a 13–6 lead in a game they would eventually lose to the San Francisco Forty-Niners by the score of 20–16.

10. CHUCK HOWLEY

Dallas Cowboys' linebacker Chuck Howley intercepted two passes and forced a fumble to earn Most Valuable Player honors in Super Bowl V. Howley holds the distinction of being the only defensive player to be named Super Bowl MVP while playing for the losing team. Despite Howley's heroics, Dallas lost to the Baltimore Colts 16–13.

INSTANT REPLAYS

Professional football has become the most-watched sport on television. The following are some of the most memorable broadcasts.

1. THE HEIDI GAME

On October 17, 1968, NBC televised a late afternoon game between the New York Jets and the Oakland Raiders. With a minute to go, New York led 32–29. Network executives decided to cut away from the game to show a children's special called *Heidi.* In the final minute, the Raiders scored two touchdowns and defeated the Jets 43–32. The NBC switchboard, unable to accommodate the volume of irate calls, blew a fuse.

2. THE ANNOUNCERLESS GAME

One of the oddest football broadcasts was an announcerless game that NBC aired on December 20, 1980. It was an experiment to test the viewers' reaction to a game without play-by-play announcers. Graphics were provided and microphones picked up the sounds on the field. Viewers found it difficult to keep track of the players and the network returned announcers to the booth for the next game. By the way, the New York Jets defeated the Miami Dolphins 24–17.

3. AHMAD RASHAD

The 1985 Thanksgiving Day broadcast of the game between the Detroit Lions and the New York Jets is remembered primarily because broadcaster and former wide receiver Ahmad Rashad proposed marriage on the air to Phylicia Ayers-Allen, star of the *Cosby Show.* Rashad nervously declared, "This is Thanksgiving Day and if she does not accept my proposal, I'll be the biggest turkey in the nation." To his relief, she accepted.

4. KEITH JACKSON

Announcer Keith Jackson's pants caught fire during the November 16, 1970, Monday Night Football broadcast of a game between the Dallas Cowboys and the St. Louis Cardinals. Jackson calmly went on with the play-by-play while dousing the flames with drinks.

5. CURT GOWDY

Curt Gowdy uttered a classic blooper during an American Football League All-Star game in the 1960s. Noting a huge puddle on the field, Gowdy observed, "If there's a pileup out there, they'll have to give some of the players artificial insemination."

6. LARRY KING

At halftime during a game between the Baltimore Colts and Miami Dolphins, announcer Larry King told viewers, "Now coming on the field to entertain is the Air Force Academy Drug and Bugle Corp."

7. **FIRST TELEVISED PROFESSIONAL FOOTBALL GAME**

NBC aired the first televised professional football game from Brooklyn's Ebbets Field on October 22, 1939. Two iconoscope cameras were used to cover the action. Because it was a cloudy day, viewers had trouble seeing the faint picture. The signal was transmitted to the 1,000 television sets in the New York area. Brooklyn defeated Philadelphia by the score of 23–14.

8. **JIM HARBAUGH**

Indianapolis Colts' quarterback Jim Harbaugh missed several weeks of the 1997 season with a broken hand following an altercation with announcer and former Buffalo Bills quarterback Jim Kelly.

9. **SUPER BOWL I**

The first Super Bowl, then known as the AFL-NFL World Championship Game, was telecast simultaneously on NBC and CBS. Due to 30,000 unsold tickets at the Memorial Coliseum, the game was blacked out in Los Angeles. A local newspaper advised fans how they could rig their antennas to pick up the signal.

10. **ROGER STAUBACH**

In response to stories about the highly active sex lives of some NFL players, straight-arrow quarterback Roger Staubach told broadcaster Phyllis George, "I enjoy sex. I just enjoy it with my wife."

OVERCOMING HANDICAPS

Many players have overcome physical handicaps and serious injuries to excel in football. As a child, NFL great Hugh McElhenny spent two years on crutches after severing tendons in his foot. Pittsburgh Steelers' running back Rocky Bleier was a 1,000-yard rusher after being injured by a grenade in Vietnam.

1. TOM DEMPSEY

Tom Dempsey was born with half a foot and a stump for a hand. Despite these handicaps, he became an outstanding place kicker. On November 8, 1970, Dempsey set an NFL record by kicking a 63-yard field goal in a game against the Detroit Lions.

2. ED BARRETT

Ed Barrett, a one-armed player, caught four passes and intercepted three in an October 31, 1930, game between Cedartown and Rome, Georgia.

3. GALLAUDET COLLEGE

In 1912, Gallaudet College, a school for the hearing impaired, played the Norfolk Blues, a team of collegiate all-stars. Norfolk, figuring that the Gallaudet players were deaf, didn't bother to huddle. What they didn't realize was that their opponents could read lips. Gallaudet, knowing what plays were coming, defeated Norfolk 20–0.

4. LARRY BROWN

Despite being almost totally deaf in his right ear, Washington Redskins' running back Larry Brown led the NFL in rushing in 1970 with 1,125 yards. For his career, Brown rushed for 5,875 yards and scored 55 touchdowns.

5. BOBBY DILLON

Defensive back Bobby Dillon lost an eye in an accident at age ten. The injury didn't stop him from becoming an All-American at Texas. As a professional, he set a Green Bay Packers' record by intercepting 52 passes from 1952 to 1959.

6. FRED ARBANAS

All-Pro Kansas City end Fred Arbanas was hit so hard in a 1965 game that his glass eye popped out. Referee Tommy Bell handed it to him and asked, "What would you do if the other eye was injured?" Arbanus replied, "I'd become a referee."

7. DUTCH CLARK

Hall of Fame tailback Dutch Clark was nearly blind in his left eye, but that didn't stop him from being selected All-NFL six times between 1931 and 1938.

8. BILLY LOTHRIDGE

Atlanta Falcons' Billy Lothridge led the NFL in punting in 1967 and 1968 despite having only one kidney. Lothridge also intercepted three passes and rushed for a touchdown.

9. JERRY KRAMER

Jerry Kramer was a starting guard for the great Green Bay Packer teams of the 1960s despite a number of serious off-the-field injuries. Kramer's hand had been sliced with an axe, his fingers injured by a shotgun blast, and his side cut by a lathe. In 1965, he had surgery to remove splinters from his intestines, the result of another childhood accident.

10. CECIL ISBELL

Cecil Isbell played quarterback for the Green Bay Packers from 1938 to 1942. During one stretch he threw touchdown passes in 23 consecutive games. Twice he led the NFL in completions, passing yardage, and touchdown passes. He did all of this despite playing his entire career with a chain attached to his body. The chain limited the motion of his left arm; if he raised the arm too high, his dislocated shoulder would pop out.

INCREDIBLE INJURIES

Injuries are common in football, but the players in this section suffered truly uncommon injuries.

1. TURK EDWARDS

Washington Redskins' tackle Turk Edwards suffered a career-ending injury during a coin toss. The Hall of Famer, known for his durability, walked to midfield for an opening coin toss prior to a September 22, 1940, game with the New York Giants. As he turned to go back to the bench, his spikes caught in the turf and injured his knee. The injury was so severe that he was forced to retire from football.

2. CLIVE RUSH

Clive Rush was hired as coach of the Boston Patriots in 1969. A press conference was called at the Hotel Somerset to introduce the new coach. As Rush stepped to the podium, his right hand touched a live microphone. Dan Marr, a minority owner of the Patriots, pulled the microphone cord out of the socket, probably saving the coach from being electrocuted. Rush collapsed but soon recovered. The inauspicious introduction was a sign of things to come. The Patriots lost their first seven games and finished Rush's first season with a 4–10 record. After another seven-game losing streak the following season, Rush was fired.

3. FRANCIS SCHMIDT

Francis Schmidt coached at Tulsa, Arkansas, Texas Christian, Ohio State, and Idaho between 1919 and 1942. Schmidt was notorious for his forgetfulness. In 1927, he was coaching at Arkansas when Oklahoma State completed a touchdown pass. Schmidt jumped up and hit his head on a recently built shelter, knocking himself out. Four years later at Texas Christian, Schmidt ran out on the field to protest a penalty. He forgot to take off his headphones and was yanked into a back flip.

4. BOB LIVINGSTON

The Notre Dame halfback was knocked senseless by one of his own teammates in a game against Illinois on September 28, 1946. End Leon Hart, playing his first game at Notre Dame, ran headfirst into the huddle. He collided with Livingston, knocking him unconscious. A few years later, Hart won the Heisman Trophy.

5. GUS FREROTTE

In 1997, Washington Redskins' quarterback Gus Frerotte knocked himself senseless by head-butting the end zone wall after scoring a touchdown.

6. GARY FALLON

Washington and Lee coach Gary Fallon was not pleased when his team trailed the University of the South 25–7 at halftime on October 23, 1987. Fallon decided that his players needed to scrimmage, even though it would interrupt the halftime festivities, including the introduction of the homecoming queen. The scrimmage proved disastrous when one of his players suffered a knee injury and another broke his leg. The extra practice didn't help their game performance either as Washington and Lee lost 38–13.

7. TOMMIE SMITH

The gold medalist in the 200-meter dash at the 1968 Olympics, Tommie Smith was one of two athletes banned after giving a Black Power salute on the medal stand. In 1969, Smith joined the Cincinnati Bengals as a wide receiver. It was thought that his great speed would make him a deep threat. Smith's first reception was for a 41-yard gain. Unfortunately, he suffered a career-ending injury on the play.

8. DAN DEVINE

On September 19, 1971, Green Bay Packers' head coach Dan Devine broke his leg in a sideline pileup in a game against the New York Giants. To add insult to injury, the Packers lost the game 42–40.

9. JOHN UNITAS

Baltimore Colts' quarterback John Unitas played through many injuries during his long tenure in pro football, but it was an off-the-field accident that ended his career. In April, 1971, Unitas tore an Achilles tendon while playing paddleball with teammate Tom Matte. Unitas was benched the following year and traded to San Diego in 1973, his final season.

10. **LIONEL TAYLOR**

Lionel Taylor led the AFL in receptions five times as a member of the Denver Broncos, but as a rookie with the Chicago Bears in 1959, he was more expendable. During a preseason game against Pittsburgh, coach George Halas summoned Taylor from the bench. "We're out of timeouts," he told the rookie. "Go out there and get hurt."

SERIOUS INJURIES

Football can be a dangerous sport.

1. DARRYL STINGLEY

One of the most tragic injuries in NFL history occurred during a 1978 game between the New England Patriots and the Oakland Raiders. Patriots' wide receiver Darryl Stingley was paralyzed after being hit hard by Oakland defensive back Jack Tatum. The 26-year-old Stingley had scored 16 touchdowns in his career.

2. MIKE UTLEY

Detroit Lions' offensive lineman Mike Utley was paralyzed with a severe neck injury during a November 17, 1991, game against the Los Angeles Rams. His teammates dedicated the season to him and went on to win a club-record 12 games.

3. DENNIS BYRD

New York Jets' defensive tackle Dennis Byrd was paralyzed after suffering a neck injury in a 1992 game against Kansas

City. The injury occurred when Byrd collided with a teammate while trying to make a tackle. After extensive therapy, Byrd was able to regain use of his legs.

4. REGGIE BROWN

Second-year Detroit linebacker Reggie Brown was badly hurt in 1997 while making a tackle. The injury was so serious that Brown nearly died on the field. In time, he was able to regain partial use of his arms and legs.

5. JOE THEISMANN

One of the ugliest injuries ever seen on television occurred in a November 18, 1985, game between the Washington Redskins and the New York Giants. Washington quarterback Joe Theismann suffered a compound fracture of his leg when he was hit by several Giant defenders. The injury was so gruesome that Giants' linebacker Lawrence Taylor frantically signaled to the sidelines for medical assistance. Theismann's extraordinary career was over.

6. STERLING SHARPE

The career of brilliant Green Bay wide receiver Sterling Sharpe ended in 1994 when he suffered a spinal injury. Sharpe led the NFL in receptions three times and twice caught more than 100 passes in a season.

7. TIM KRUMRIE

During the first quarter of Super Bowl XXIII, Cincinnati Bengals' defensive tackle Tim Krumrie caught his left foot in the turf while attempting to tackle San Francisco Forty-Niners' running back Roger Craig. Krumrie broke his leg in two places.

Jon SooHoo

Sterling Sharpe

Sharpe, one of the league's best receivers in the early 1990s, had his career cut short by a spinal injury.

The gruesome injury was replayed over and over again for the TV audience. The Bengals, without their All-Pro tackle, lost 20–16.

8. FRANK GIFFORD

In a 1960 game against the Philadelphia Eagles, New York Giants' halfback Frank Gifford suffered an injury that nearly ended his career. Gifford was running a down-and-in pattern when he took a vicious hit from Philadelphia linebacker Chuck Bednarik. Gifford's skull was fractured, and he missed the rest of the 1960 season and the entire 1961 season.

9. GALE SAYERS

Gale Sayers may have been the greatest all-around back in pro football history. Sayers scored 22 touchdowns in his rookie season with the Chicago Bears in 1965. His career was shortened when he suffered a knee injury in 1968 while being tackled by San Francisco Forty-Niners defensive back Kermit Alexander.

10. CRAZY LEGS HIRSCH

End Elroy "Crazy Legs" Hirsch had his skull fractured while playing for Chicago of the All-American Football Conference in 1948. After the injury, his legs seemed to zigzag out of control. The unorthodox running style apparently confused defenders, and Crazy Legs became one of the NFL's most feared receivers.

TOUGH GUYS

Football is not a game for sissies. The following players were especially tough.

1. JIM OTTO

Jim Otto never missed a game in his 15 years with the Oakland Raiders. He played in 210 consecutive games from 1960 to 1974 despite ten broken noses, numerous knee injuries, and more than 30 surgeries. The 12-time All-Pro center was described by an opponent as "tougher than an old boot."

2. LARRY WILSON

The man who invented the safety blitz, Larry Wilson played for the St. Louis Cardinals from 1960 to 1972. During his career, the Hall of Famer intercepted 52 passes, but it was one particular interception in 1965 that has become part of football lore. Wilson, who insisted on playing despite wearing casts on both of his broken hands, intercepted a Bill Nelsen pass and returned it 35 yards. Quarterback Bobby Layne said Wilson was "pound for pound the toughest player in the NFL."

3. MIKE CURTIS

Nicknamed the "Animal," Baltimore Colts linebacker Mike Curtis was so tough that he chewed the bars off his face mask. He once ate the window panes of the team bus. In practice, none of his teammates was safe from his wrath. On December 11, 1971, in a game against the Miami Dolphins, Curtis knocked unconscious a fan who made the mistake of running onto the field. Curtis admitted that he played football because it was the only way he could hit someone and get away with it.

4. JOHNNY UNITAS

Johnny Unitas was arguably the greatest quarterback in pro football history and certainly among the toughest. Over the years he played through a number of injuries, including broken fingers, ripped arm tendons, and torn knee cartilage. In 1958, with broken ribs and a punctured lung, he led the Colts to the NFL title while wearing a protective harness. Two years later Unitas played the entire season with a broken vertebrae.

5. ERNIE NEVERS

Ernie Nevers' performance in the 1925 Rose Bowl demonstrated his toughness. The Stanford halfback broke one ankle in 1924 and the other late in the 1925 season. With both ankles heavily taped, Nevers rushed for 114 yards and made most of his team's tackles in a 27–10 loss to Notre Dame.

6. ACE PARKER

Brooklyn tailback Ace Parker played from 1937 to 1945. The 165-pounder once ran for a 60-yard touchdown against the

Chicago Bears while wearing aluminum casts to protect his injured legs.

7. JIM MARSHALL

Minnesota Vikings' defensive lineman Jim Marshall holds the NFL record with 282 consecutive games played. He maintained the streak despite pneumonia, an ulcer, and a shotgun wound to his side.

8. JOE KAPP

Quarterback Joe Kapp of the Minnesota Vikings said, "Football is an animal game. I am an animal." In a 1969 contest against Cleveland, Kapp was carried off the field on a stretcher after being leveled by linebacker Jim Houston. Kapp returned and threw a 20-yard touchdown to halfback Bill Brown. In another game against the Detroit Lions, Kapp was knocked out, but finished the game after backup quarterback Gary Cuozzo broke his collarbone.

9. FREDERIC REMINGTON

Some people wear their toughness on their sleeve. Frederic Remington wore it on his entire uniform. Prior to an 1879 game with Princeton, the Yale end dipped his uniform in animal blood "to make it look more businesslike." Remington later became a famed painter and sculptor of frontier scenes.

10. DAN DIERDORF

In 1977, All-Pro St. Louis Cardinals' offensive lineman Dan Dierdorf played several games with a broken jaw. Dierdorf wore a specially padded helmet.

HARD HITTERS

When these guys hit you, you knew it.

1. HARDY BROWN

At 193 pounds, Hardy Brown was an undersized linebacker, but no one ever tackled with such force. In 1951, Brown knocked out 21 players. In a game with the Washington Redskins, he disabled the entire backfield one by one. "Hardy the Hatchet" broke more noses and jaws than any other player. Cleveland Browns' halfback Billy Reynolds was hospitalized for four days after a Brown hit. On the final play before halftime in a game against Los Angeles, Brown decked Rams' fullback Dick Hoerner and both teams left the field without noticing Hoerner still prone on the ground. When the players returned to the field for the second half, they discovered Hoerner trying to get to his feet. The Rams put a bounty on Brown's head but no one was able to take him out of action. Brown would crouch and then spring into the ballcarrier, driving his shoulder under his opponent's chin. Teams suspected that his shoulder pads were loaded but officials never found anything illegal. Quarterback Y.A. Tittle said of Brown, "He may have been the hardest hitter who ever played. He just exploded through people."

2. JACK TATUM

Raiders' defensive back Jack "The Assassin" Tatum hit so hard that he sometimes knocked out his own teammates who were assisting on a tackle. His hit on Pittsburgh halfback Frenchy Fuqua caused the ball to fly in the air, allowing Franco Harris to make the "Immaculate Reception." In 1978, Tatum paralyzed Patriots' receiver Darryl Stingley.

3. ED SPRINKLE

Chicago Bears' defensive end Ed "Nose Breaker" Sprinkle earned his nickname. Sprinkle terrorized ballcarriers from 1944 to 1955. Bears coach George Halas called him "the greatest pass rusher I've ever seen." *Sport* magazine named him "The Meanest Man in Football." One of his ferocious hits broke Cleveland quarterback Otto Graham's nose, knocked off his helmet, and caused a fumble. Sprinkle picked up the fumble and ran 55 yards for a touchdown. Sprinkle hit halfback Hugh McElhenny so hard that it turned McElhenny's helmet around. In a 1946 game against the New York Giants, Sprinkle broke the noses of two players and separated the shoulder of another.

4. ZANY ZATKOFF

Roger "Zany" Zatkoff played linebacker and defensive end for Green Bay and Detroit from 1953 to 1958. Zatkoff was such a powerful hitter that teammates put a cowbell on him so they wouldn't be blindsided in practice. One of his favorite moves was to spear opponents in the chest with his helmet. Zatkoff kept a count of the number of players that he knocked out of games. It was not uncommon for him to take out two or three players at a time.

5. NIGHT TRAIN LANE

It was said that defensive back Dick "Night Train" Lane hit like a locomotive. He grabbed ballcarriers around the head in a "ring neck" tackle. His flagrant use of clotheslining and grabbing the face mask brought about rules changes that outlawed these practices.

6. FRED "THE HAMMER" WILLIAMSON

Defensive back Fred Williamson was called "The Hammer" because he frequently used forearm shots to level receivers. The Hammer broke Howard Twilley's cheekbone and Frank Jackson's nose. Prior to Super Bowl I, the Kansas City cornerback promised, "Two hammers for Boyd Dowler and one for Carroll Dale." Despite threatening the Green Bay receivers, it was Williamson who was knocked cold during the game.

7. BRONKO NAGURSKI

Bronko Nagurski was more dangerous on offense than most players are on defense. In his first day of practice at the University of Minnesota, Bronko knocked loose the tackling dummy. As a professional, he knocked out four would-be tacklers on a kickoff return. New York Giants' coach Steve Owen said of Nagurski, "He was the only back I ever saw who ran his own interference." Green Bay fullback Clarke Hinkle warned, "You better get out of his way or he'll kill you."

8. DICK BUTKUS

Chicago Bears' linebacker Dick Butkus usually stopped ballcarriers dead in their tracks. Butkus hit Pittsburgh center Ray

Mansfield so hard that Mansfield stumbled over and sat on the Bears' bench by mistake. O.J. Simpson said, "Butkus doesn't want to hurt you. He wants to kill you." Butkus said that he never tried to hurt anyone, unless it was an important game.

9. FRANK HINKLEY

An All-American end at Yale from 1891 to 1893, Frank Hinkley was the most feared tackler of his time. Walter Camp wrote that Hinkley "drifted through interference like a disembodied spirit." The 155-pound Hinkley was described as cadaverous-looking and playing like a fiend. He grabbed ballcarriers around the knees, picked them up, and drove them headfirst into the ground. Harvard players were so appalled by his rough style that they refused to play Yale for a year.

10. RONNIE LOTT

Ronnie Lott of the San Francisco Forty-Niners and New York Jets was a defensive back who hit with the power of a linebacker. The ten-time Pro Bowler intimidated receivers to such an extent that they listened for his footsteps. Once, when Lott broke a finger during a game, he cut off the tip of his broken finger rather than sit out the rest of the game.

PERSONAL FOULS

These men sometimes played dirty.

1. CONRAD DOBLER

Conrad Dobler was an offensive lineman who played from 1972 to 1981. Many believe that he was the most offensive player in pro football history. Alex Karras called him "the dirtiest player in football" and few disagreed. Dobler admitted that he spent the week before a game building hatred for his opponent. Among Dobler's principal offenses were biting, gouging, punching, kicking, and grabbing the face mask. In 1974, he used a cast on his broken left hand as a weapon. Dobler punched Pittsburgh's Mean Joe Greene in the solar plexus and kicked the Rams' Merlin Olsen in the head. He spit in the face of Eagles' safety Bill Bradley as he lay injured on the ground. When Giants' defensive tackle Jim Pietrzak wished him good luck in the playoffs, Dobler punched him. He bit one tackle so many times that the player requested a rabies shot. Dobler claimed that if he hit someone after the whistle, it was because of bad timing. He swore that he would never intentionally blind anyone, only blur their vision.

2. GEORGE TRAFTON

Red Grange called George Trafton "the toughest, meanest, most ornery critter alive." The 235-pound center, known as "The Brute," was considered the dirtiest player of his time. Expelled from Notre Dame, Trafton saved his roughest play for the pros. As a rookie with the Decatur Staleys in 1920, he so angered the Rock Island Independents that they sent four players into the game on a mission to injure Trafton. Within 12 minutes, all four players had been knocked out of the game by The Brute. He broke the leg and ended the career of tailback Fred Chicken by throwing him into a fence. The Rock Island fans were so outraged that a rock-throwing mob chased him from the field.

3. BITER JONES

Guard Biter Jones made the All Missouri Valley team three years in a row. When he wasn't blocking players, he was biting them. According to his coach, Jones bit at least 14 players.

4. MEAN JOE GREENE

Pittsburgh Steelers defensive tackle Joe Greene wasn't called "Mean" for nothing. His specialty was kicking a player when he was down. In a 1975 game against Cleveland, Greene was ejected for repeatedly kicking Browns' guard Bob McKay in the groin.

5. JOHNNY SAMPLE

Johnny Sample was an outstanding defensive back for the Colts, Steelers, Redskins, and Jets from 1958 to 1968. The title of his autobiography, *Confessions of a Dirty Ballplayer,* described his approach to the game. He once told Frank Gifford, "I'm going to mess up your face."

6. LES RICHTER

Les Richter was a Los Angeles Rams' linebacker who didn't shy away from rough play. One of his victims said, "If a mugger in Central Park at night did what Richter does in the afternoon, even the other muggers would turn him in."

7. BILL ROMANOWSKI

Bill Romanowski has been fined numerous times by the NFL for unnecessary roughness. On August 9, 1997, the Broncos' linebacker broke Carolina Panthers' quarterback Kerry Collins' jaw with a helmet-to-helmet hit.

8. TANK YOUNGER

Paul "Tank" Younger was one of the first African-American stars of professional football. He was known for his all-out brutal play. George Halas told him, "Tank, you're the greatest, dirtiest, best football player in the league."

9. JEROME WOODS

Prior to a 1997 game against Denver, Kansas City Chiefs' coach Marty Schottenheimer allegedly offered to pay any fines his players might incur for breaking the jaws of Broncos players. Although no jaws were broken, safety Jerome Woods was fined $10,000 for a head shot to wide receiver Ed McCaffrey, whose face was bloodied.

10. WOODY HAYES

Ohio State coach Woody Hayes ended an illustrious career with one of the most flagrant cheap shots in football history. At the end of the 1978 Gator Bowl, Clemson linebacker Charlie

Bauman intercepted a Buckeye pass to seal a 17–15 Clemson victory. Bauman was knocked out of bounds on the Ohio State sidelines when Coach Hayes punched him in the throat. Hayes had to be subdued by his own players, and he was fired the next day.

BENDING THE RULES

These individuals broke the rules—or at least bent them a little.

1. TOMMY LEWIS

In the 1954 Cotton Bowl, Alabama was unable to stop Rice's running back Dicky Moegle. He rushed for 265 yards on just 11 carries, an average of more than 24 yards per rushing attempt. Early in the second quarter, Moegle ran for a 79-yard touchdown. Later in the period he broke loose from his own five-yard line and raced down the sidelines for another apparent touchdown. As he ran past the Crimson Tide players on the sidelines, fullback Tommy Lewis, unable to restrain himself, leaped off the bench and tackled Moegle at the Alabama 40-yard line. The officials credited Moegle with a 95-yard touchdown run, and Rice won the game 28–6.

2. POP WARNER

Carlisle coach Pop Warner had a bag of tricks that he used whenever he could get away with it. In a 1903 game against Syracuse, Warner had football-shaped patches sewn onto his team's uniforms to confuse defenses. The next week against Harvard, Warner used a hidden-ball trick to score a touchdown.

3. ALONZO AWTREY

Georgia coach W.A. Cunningham found a unique way to fool Alabama on October 26, 1912. On the first play of the game, flanker Alonzo Awtrey stood near the sidelines, dressed in white coveralls and holding a bucket. The Alabama players assumed he was the water boy until quarterback Timon Bowden threw him a pass for a long gain. Alabama fans were so angered by the deception that a riot ensued. Georgia won the game 13–9.

4. FRANK LEAHY

Notre Dame coach Frank Leahy pulled the same trick not once, but twice in a game against Iowa on November 21, 1953. With two seconds left in the first half and trailing 7–0, Leahy had tackle Frank Varrichone pretend to faint in order to stop the clock on an injury time-out. The Irish took advantage of the ruse and scored a touchdown on the last play of the half. Behind 14–7 in the closing seconds, Leahy instructed two more players to collapse. Notre Dame again took advantage of the ensuing time-out and scored the tying touchdown with six seconds left. The NCAA subsequently changed its rules so that teams could not fake injuries to stop the clock.

5. RON MEYER

Ron Meyer, coach of the New England Patriots, pulled a snow job on Don Shula and the Miami Dolphins on December 12, 1982. The game was played at New England on a field covered with snow. With 55 seconds remaining and the score tied 0–0, kicker John Smith of the Patriots lined up for a game-winning 33-yard field goal. At that moment, a snow sweeper was brought out to clear the line of scrimmage. The sweeper was operated by Mark Henderson, a convicted burglar who was on a work-release program from the Norfolk Correctional Institute. As he crossed the field, Henderson veered several yards to clear the spot where Smith would kick the ball. Smith subsequently kicked the game-winning field goal. Asked after the game about his participation in this bit of football larceny, Henderson replied, "What are they going to do? Put me in jail?"

6. CHUCK MEEHAN

Maryland's star kicker Ed Brewer had punts of 72 and 60 yards and kicked a game-winning 36-yard field goal in a 1920 game against Syracuse. Determined not to be beaten by Brewer again, Syracuse coach Chuck Meehan deflated the footballs Brewer kicked in the rematch played on October 8, 1921. As a result, Brewer missed all three field-goal attempts and punted for a 20-yard average in a 42–0 loss to the Orangemen.

7. SAM MCALLESTER

Alabama players may have wondered why Tennessee fullback Sam McAllester wore leather loops on his belt for their November 24, 1904, game. They soon found out. On each play, the Caldwell brothers, two strong Tennessee halfbacks, grabbed the loops and hurled McAllester over the line of scrimmage. This unorthodox approach to the running game resulted in consistent gains, and McAllester scored the contest's only touchdown.

8. SAMMY GROSS

Iowa quarterback Sammy Gross pulled off a one-of-a-kind quarterback sneak on November 8, 1914, against Northwestern. Throughout the game, Gross complained about nonexistent penalties. Finally, in the fourth quarter, at his own 16-yard line, Gross told the referee that if he wasn't going to call the penalty, then Gross would walk off the 15 yards himself. While everyone stood and watched, Gross began pacing off the imaginary penalty. Only after he crossed the line of scrimmage did he begin to run. Before Northwestern realized that they had been tricked, Gross gained 54 yards. Iowa won the game by the score of 27–0.

9. GEORGE ALLEN

George Allen, coach of the Washington Redskins, was once accused by a rival coach of spying on his practices. He charged that Allen hired a woman to push a baby cart near the practice field. The coach believed that a midget was hidden in the cart, taking notes on the practice.

10. J.V. KING

No one could accuse reporter J.V. King of being unbiased. King had played football for Colgate and was reporting the 1897 game against Syracuse. With the score tied 6–6, Syracuse's Haden Patten was running down the sidelines on his way to an apparent touchdown when King ran onto the field and tackled him. Thanks to King's interference, the game ended in a 6–6 tie.

IT'S A GAMBLE

Football and gambling have always had a connection. Each year millions of dollars are wagered both legally and illegally on the sport. The point spread is as important to some people as which team wins the game. The problem of betting on football was brilliantly satirized by E.B. White in his parable, "The Decline of Sport." In the story, one bettor, overwhelmed by too many gambling disappointments, shot a football player just as he was about to score a touchdown.

1. ART SCHLICHTER

The story of quarterback Art Schlichter shows how compulsive gambling can destroy a promising career. During his years at Ohio State, Schlichter seemed like such an all-American boy that his biography was titled, *Straight Arrow*. In fact, he was already in debt to gamblers for thousands of dollars when he was still in college. Drafted in the first round by the Baltimore Colts in 1982, Schlichter lost his entire $350,000 signing bonus and $140,000 salary to gamblers. As a professional, Schlichter threw only three touchdown passes and was out of the league by 1985. Never able to kick his gambling addiction, Schlichter was charged with mail fraud for writing nearly a half million dollars in bad checks, and served prison time in Indiana in 1995. In May, 2000, he was arrested and charged with money laundering and fraud.

2. ALEX KARRAS

Two of the NFL's biggest stars, Detroit defensive tackle Alex Karras and Green Bay halfback Paul Hornung, were suspended in 1963 for one year for gambling on football. Karras spent his year off as a professional wrestler. When he returned, he was asked by an official to call "heads or tails" during a coin toss. Karras declined, saying, "I'm sorry, sir. I'm not permitted to gamble."

3. FRANK FILCHOCK

Prior to the 1946 NFL Championship Game between New York and the Chicago Bears, Giants' quarterback Frank Filchock and fullback Merle Hapes were under investigation for an alleged bribery attempt. Supposedly, the players had been offered $2,500 each to lose the game by more than the ten-point spread. Hapes admitted only to receiving the bribe offer and was barred from playing in the championship game by NFL Commissioner Bert Bell. Filchock denied his involvement and was permitted to participate. He played despite a broken nose, but threw six interceptions in a 24–14 loss to the Bears. Filchock subsequently admitted to receiving the bribe offer as well and never played for the Giants again. Four years later, he appeared in one game for the Baltimore Colts. Hapes never played in another NFL game. There was no evidence either man accepted a bribe.

4. **ART ROONEY**

The long-time owner of the Pittsburgh Steelers was an astute horse bettor. In one Saratoga race, he won more than $350,000. Rooney purchased the Steelers in 1933 with $2,500 he had won that day betting on horses.

5. **TIM MARA**

Tim Mara was a bookmaker who bought the New York Giants franchise in 1925 for $500. Mara had no interest in football at the time but figured any New York franchise was worth a $500 investment.

6. **LEONARD TOSE**

It was rumored that Philadelphia Eagles owner Leonard Tose lost millions of dollars at the gambling tables of Las Vegas and Atlantic City.

7. **EDWARD DEBARTOLO JR.**

Edward DeBartolo Jr. owned the San Francisco Forty-Niners team that won five Super Bowls between 1982 and 1995. He gave up control of the team after a federal fraud investigation accused him of illegally securing a riverboat casino license in Louisiana.

8. **SHIPWRECK KELLY**

John "Shipwreck" Kelly, a Brooklyn tailback in the 1930s, had a leopard-skin poker table in his house. He played high-stakes poker games with his millionaire friends, each chip worth $10,000.

9. JIM THORPE

The Canton Bulldogs and Massillon Tigers were scheduled to meet for the 1916 Ohio League championship. In the lobby of the Courtland Hotel, a Massillon supporter bragged that he would bet anyone $2,500 that Massillon would beat Canton. Canton's star player, Jim Thorpe, accepted the bet. Canton won the game, and Thorpe's gambling winnings were more than his annual salary. At the time he was receiving $250 a game.

10. JOE NAMATH

In 1965, New York Jets quarterback Joe Namath was ordered by the league to sell his holdings in a New York nightclub, Brothers III, because it was reportedly frequented by gamblers. Namath refused and temporarily retired from football. Later, he changed his mind.

ILLEGAL SUBSTANCES

Unfortunately, many NFL players have been victims of substance abuse.

1. GENE "BIG DADDY" LIPSCOMB

Gene "Big Daddy" Lipscomb was a four-time All-Pro defensive lineman with the Baltimore Colts. In May, 1963, Lipscomb was found dead from an apparent heroin overdose. He was 31 years old.

2. DON ROGERS

Defensive back Don Rogers of the Cleveland Browns died from a cocaine overdose on June 27, 1986. The former UCLA star was only 23 years old.

3. MERCURY MORRIS

Running back Mercury Morris gained more than 4,000 yards during his NFL career, which lasted from 1969 to 1976. In 1982, Morris was arrested for selling cocaine and served three years in prison.

4. DEXTER MANLEY

Few players' struggles with substance abuse were as highly publicized as that of defensive end Dexter Manley. Playing for the Washington Redskins from 1980 to 1989, he was one of the best defensive linemen in the game. In 1991, Manley was banned from the NFL for failing a drug test for the fourth time.

5. BAM MORRIS

Bam Morris was a hard-hitting running back for the Steelers, Colts, Bears, and Chiefs from 1994 to 1998. In July, 1996, he pleaded guilty to possession of five pounds of marijuana.

6. DUANE THOMAS

Duane Thomas seemed on his way to an outstanding pro career with the Dallas Cowboys. In 1971, the second-year running back rushed for a league-leading 11 touchdowns. Thomas gained 95 yards and scored a touchdown in Dallas' 24–3 victory over Miami in Super Bowl VI. Shortly after the Super Bowl, Thomas was pulled over by law officials in Texas who found marijuana in his automobile. Thomas pleaded guilty and was sentenced to five years' probation. Traded by the Cowboys to Washington, Thomas was out of football by 1974.

7. CHUCK MUNCIE

On September 10, 1984, San Diego Chargers' running back Chuck Muncie was suspended from the NFL for a year after failing a drug test. The two-time 1,000-yard rusher never appeared in another NFL game.

8. LAWRENCE TAYLOR

The man who many call the greatest defensive player in NFL history, Lawrence Taylor was a ten-time Pro-Bowl linebacker with the New York Giants. In October, 1998, Taylor was charged with possession of crack cocaine and drug paraphernalia. In November, 1999, he pleaded no contest to buying crack cocaine from an undercover policeman in St. Petersburg Beach, Florida.

9. PETE JOHNSON

Cincinnati Bengals' running back Pete Johnson and defensive end Ross Browner were suspended for the first four games of the 1983 season for testing positive for drugs.

10. HOLLYWOOD HENDERSON

Dallas Cowboys' linebacker Thomas "Hollywood" Henderson admitted that he was often high during games. He later reformed his ways and, in 1985, he began counseling drug and alcohol abusers in Austin, Texas.

CRIME AND FOOTBALL

One study indicated that over 20 percent of players then in the NFL had been charged with serious crimes. The league began addressing the problem in 2000 after player Rae Carruth was charged with murder.

1. O.J. SIMPSON

The 1995 murder trial of former NFL great O.J. Simpson was called the Trial of the Century. Simpson was accused in the double murder of his ex-wife, Nicole, and Ron Goldman. In a controversial decision, Simpson was acquitted in the murder trial, but later found liable in a civil suit. One of the items that was auctioned to settle the suit was Simpson's Heisman Trophy.

2. JIM TYRER

An All-Pro for ten consecutive years with the Kansas City Chiefs, offensive tackle Jim Tyrer retired in 1974. Six years later, depressed over bad business deals, Tyrer killed his wife and then committed suicide.

3. RAE CARRUTH

Wide receiver Rae Carruth caught 44 passes as a rookie with the Carolina Panthers in 1997. He was arrested following the November 16, 1999, drive-by shooting of his pregnant girlfriend, Cherica Adams. When Adams died a month later, Carruth and three co-defendants were charged with first-degree murder. Carruth maintained his innocence, and the case had not gone to trial at the time this was written.

4. DARRYL HENLEY

Darryl Henley played cornerback for the Los Angeles Rams from 1989 to 1994. Following his playing career, he was convicted of soliciting the murder of a federal judge. He was sentenced to 41 years in the Marion Federal Prison for his involvement in the murder-for-hire plot and for drug trafficking.

5. LEWIS BILLUPS

Lewis Billups was a defensive back with the Cincinnati Bengals from 1986 to 1991. Billups served time after threatening to break NBA star Rex Chapman's legs in a dispute concerning Chapman's sister. He also pleaded guilty for sexually assaulting a woman in Florida while another man videotaped it. A girlfriend of Billups claimed she had to endure seven plastic surgeries on her face following a beating. Billups died in an automobile accident in Florida in April, 1994.

6. REGGIE ROGERS

Detroit Lions' defensive end Reggie Rogers was convicted of vehicular homicide in an accident which occurred on October 20, 1988. Three occupants of the other car were killed, and Rogers suffered a fractured neck. Rogers served 16 months in a Michigan penitentiary.

Jon SooHoo

Randy Moss

Despite being a top prospect, Randy Moss was not drafted until late in the first round of the 1998 NFL draft because of concerns about past trouble with the law. The Vikings' selection of Moss with the 21st pick was a steal, and the rookie helped his team to a 15–1 record that year by catching 17 touchdown passes.

7. KEITH HENDERSON

In his best season, running back Keith Henderson rushed for 561 yards for the 1991 San Francisco Forty-Niners. After Henderson was released by the Minnesota Vikings in 1993, he was charged and convicted in the rape of three women.

8. BARRY SWITZER

Dallas Cowboys' head coach Barry Switzer was arrested on August 8, 1997, and charged with carrying a concealed weapon, a .38 caliber pistol, in his luggage. He was sentenced to one-year probation, fined $3,500, and required to do 80-hours community service. Cowboys' owner Jerry Jones also fined Switzer $75,000.

9. BILLY CANNON

Louisiana State University halfback Billy Cannon won the Heisman Trophy in 1959. As a professional, he led the AFL in rushing with the Houston Oilers in 1961. In July 1983, Cannon pleaded guilty to involvement in a counterfeiting scam.

10. RANDY MOSS

Randy Moss was convicted of attacking a youth when Moss was in high school in West Virginia. Although he was considered one of the best players in the 1998 NFL draft, Moss wasn't selected until the 21st pick because of his past troubles with the law. The wide receiver immediately justified the Minnesota Vikings' faith with 17 touchdown receptions as a rookie.

FANATICS

Football fans are among the most rabid in sports. The fans in the following list showed their enthusiasm in unusual—and sometimes shocking—fashion.

1. AUBURN FANS

The Georgia Tech football team was in for a surprise when it arrived by train for a November 7, 1896, game against Auburn. Auburn fans had greased the railroad track so the train was not able to stop until it was five miles past the station. The Georgia Tech players were forced to walk back to town while carrying their heavy equipment. The exhausted Yellow Jackets were trounced by Auburn 45–0. It was believed that Auburn coach John Heisman masterminded the prank.

2. RAINCOAT MAN

In November, 1961, the Dallas Texans played the Boston Patriots at Boston University's Nickerson Field. The Patriots led 28–21 with 25 seconds left and Dallas five yards away from tying the score. Quarterback Cotton Davidson threw a pass toward receiver Chris Burford. At the last second, a man in a raincoat knocked the ball out of Burford's hands. The referees somehow didn't see the fan's interference, and the Patriots won the game.

3. CLEMSON STUDENTS

The Clemson-South Carolina rivalry is one of the most intense in college football, but it took a nasty turn in their 1946 game. A counterfeiter had printed up 10,000 bogus tickets, causing a riot. Angry fans crashed the gates and stood five deep around the field. During halftime, two Clemson students plucked the Gamecock mascot and wrung its neck in front of the horrified crowd.

4. DALLAS COWBOY FANS

For their opening game on September 24, 1960, the Dallas Cowboys invited Roy Rogers to make a special appearance at halftime. The King of the Cowboys didn't get the reception he had expected. While he was being driven around the field in a Cadillac convertible, unruly fans pelted him with ice and anything else they could throw. Forty-three fans were arrested in the disturbance.

5. TENNESSEE FAN

For one Tennessee fan, football was a matter of life and death. Tennessee and Georgia were locked in a scoreless tie on October 24, 1908. When the Bulldogs lined up at the two-yard line, on the verge of scoring, a Tennessee fan stepped from the sidelines with a revolver and threatened to shoot anyone who crossed the goal line. Police arrested the man, but the Georgia quarterback was so shaken that he fumbled on the next play. Georgia was shut out by Tennessee 10–0.

6. UMBRELLA WOMAN

Giants' captain Ray Flaherty found himself under attack from a surprising source in a game against Staten Island in the early 1930s. Staten Island fullback Ken Strong was running around end when Flaherty tried to tackle him near the sidelines. Making Flaherty's job more difficult was a little old woman who reached over a fence and hit him repeatedly across the head with an umbrella.

7. DAWG POUND

Cleveland Browns' fans were among the most vocal in the NFL. Strong supporters of their team, the inhabitants of the Dawg Pound were known to throw dog biscuits, bones, eggs, and batteries at opposing players.

8. BUFFALO FANS

Place kicker Booth Lusteg learned the hard way that Buffalo fans don't appreciate missed field-goal attempts. On October 16, 1966, Lusteg flubbed a 23-yard field goal, costing the Bills a victory against San Diego. After the game, Lusteg was sitting in his car when he was approached by four fans. "Are you Booth Lusteg?" one of them asked. When Lusteg admitted who he was, one of the men punched him in the nose.

9. MINNESOTA FANS

Coach Murray Warmath's University of Minnesota teams experienced some lean years in the late 1950s. Minnesota won only one game in 1958 and just two in 1959. Some of the alumni decided to take matters into their own hands. Warmath received anonymous calls offering him bribes to resign. Even worse, there were threats against his children. The threats ended in 1960 when Minnesota won the Big Ten title and defeated UCLA 21–3 in the Rose Bowl.

10. NEW YORK JETS FANS

After a 37–14 defeat by Buffalo on October 17, 1988, some New York Jets fans set fires in the stands at Shea Stadium. Fifteen people were arrested before order was restored.

DEATH IN THE AFTERNOON

Football can be a brutal game. Sometimes it can even be fatal. Before headgear was mandatory, hundreds of players were killed on the field. In 1905, President Theodore Roosevelt threatened to ban the game if safety measures weren't enacted.

1. THE PACIFIC GLASS WORKS TRAGEDY

The largest death toll at a football game occurred when Stanford met California on November 29, 1900. Hundreds of fans were watching the action from the roof of the Pacific Glass Works located next to the stadium. The weight of the crowd caused the roof to collapse, plunging bodies into vats of molten glass. Thirteen people died in the tragedy.

2. CHUCK HUGHES

Chuck Hughes, a 28-year-old receiver with the Detroit Lions, collapsed and died from a heart attack during an October 24, 1971, game against the Chicago Bears.

3. HOWARD GLENN

Howard Glenn, a rookie guard with the New York Titans, suffered a broken neck in an October 9, 1960, game against the Houston Oilers. Glenn died later that day.

4. MACK LEE HILL

During his two-year career with the Kansas City Chiefs, fullback Mack Lee Hill averaged an impressive 5.2 yards per carry. The 25-year-old died on the operating table on December 14, 1965, while undergoing routine knee surgery to repair an injury he had suffered in a game.

5. EUGENE BYRNE

Army captain Eugene Byrne collapsed and died after tackling Harvard fullback Dodo Monot in a 1909 game.

6. STONE JOHNSON

Kansas City rookie running back Stone Johnson suffered a fatal injury in a preseason game against the Houston Oilers in 1963. The 14th-round draft choice from Grambling broke his neck while attempting to block on a kickoff return.

7. STAN MAULDIN

Stan Mauldin, the Chicago Cardinals' All-Pro tackle, collapsed from a heart attack in the locker room following the season opener against the Philadelphia Eagles on September 24, 1948. Mauldin died the next day.

8. FRANK BUNCOM

A three-time AFL All-Star, linebacker Frank Buncom died of a pulmonary embolism in his hotel room hours before the

1969 Cincinnati Bengals season opener against the Miami Dolphins.

9. J.V. CAIN

St. Louis Cardinals' tight end J.V. Cain suffered heart failure during training camp. He was attempting a comeback after missing the entire 1978 season with a torn Achilles tendon. Cain died on July 22, 1979, his 28th birthday.

10. BERT BELL

Bert Bell, the 64-year-old commissioner of the NFL, died of a heart attack while watching a game between the Philadelphia Eagles and Pittsburgh Steelers on October 11, 1959.

DEAD BEFORE THEIR TIMES

Although none of these players died as the result of football injuries, they all died too young.

1. MARSHALL UNIVERSITY

The worst football-related tragedy occurred on November 14, 1970, when 37 members of the Marshall University football team perished in a plane crash near Kenova, West Virginia.

2. WICHITA STATE

Fourteen Wichita State players were killed in an airplane crash near Denver on October 2, 1970. The team was flying to Utah for a game against Utah State. The surviving players insisted on finishing the season but lost the remaining six games.

3. CAL POLY—SAN LUIS OBISPO

The Cal Poly–San Luis Obispo Mustangs lost to Bowling Green 50–6 in a game played on October 29, 1960. A bad day turned tragic when their plane crashed on takeoff in Toledo,

Ohio, killing 16 members of the team. The next year Bowling Green played Fresno State in the Mercy Bowl, which raised money for the victims of the crash.

4. JEFF ALM

Jeff Alm, a fourth-year defensive lineman for the Houston Oilers, committed suicide on December 14, 1993, at the age of 25.

5. BRIAN PICCOLO

Running back Brian Piccolo played four seasons with the Chicago Bears. Stricken with cancer, he died on June 16, 1970, at the age of 26. A memorable movie, *Brian's Song,* was based on his life and friendship with teammate Gale Sayers.

6. DERRICK THOMAS

Kansas City Chiefs' fans were stunned when their perennial All-Pro linebacker Derrick Thomas died from injuries sustained in an automobile accident in 2000. Thomas was a fan-favorite who was revered for his fearsome defensive play and his community service work in the Kansas City area. The 33-year-old ranked among the all-time NFL leaders in quarterback sacks.

7. GEORGE GIPP

George Gipp was an All-American halfback at Notre Dame. His school career rushing mark stood for nearly 60 years. Gipp died from pneumonia on December 4, 1920, at the age of 25. Eight years later, Notre Dame coach Knute Rockne's "Let's win one for the Gipper" speech immortalized Gipp.

Jon SooHoo

Derrick Thomas

The Chiefs' future Hall-of-Fame linebacker, known for his fierce pass-rushing skills, died in February, 2000, of complications from injuries sustained in an automobile accident.

8. AL BLOZIS

Al Blozis played tackle for the New York Giants from 1942 to 1944. Two games into the 1944 season, Blozis entered the military service. On January 31, 1945, Lieutenant Blozis' patrol was fighting in the Vosges Mountains in France. When some of his men didn't return, Blozis walked into a snowstorm to try to find them. He never returned.

9. WILLIE GALIMORE

Halfback Willie Galimore gained nearly 3,000 yards in his career with the Chicago Bears from 1957 to 1963. Galimore and Bears' wide receiver Bo Farrington were killed in an automobile accident in Indiana on July 26, 1964.

10. TROY ARCHER

Troy Archer, a starting defensive tackle for the New York Giants, was killed in an automobile accident in New Jersey on June 22, 1979. Archer was about to begin his fourth season with the Giants.

OUT WITH A BANG

Most players retire past their prime, but these athletes saved their best for last.

1. JIM BROWN

Jim Brown retired after the 1965 season to pursue an acting career. In his final season, the Cleveland running back led the NFL in rushing with 1,544 yards—no surprise, since Brown had led the league eight of his nine years as a professional.

2. SONNY JURGENSEN

Life began at 40 for Washington Redskins' quarterback Sonny Jurgensen. In 1974, the 40-year-old, one of the best pure passers in pro football history, led the league in passing. Jurgensen completed 64.1 percent of his passes and earned a 94.5 quarterback rating.

3. ROGER STAUBACH

Quarterback Roger Staubach had his greatest season in 1979, his 11th and final campaign with the Dallas Cowboys. He led the National Football League in passing for the second consecutive year and notched career highs in completions, passing yards, and touchdown passes.

4. CECIL ISBELL

Green Bay Packers' quarterback Cecil Isbell retired after the 1942 season. In his final year, he led the NFL in completions, passing yards, and touchdown passes.

5. CLIFF BATTLES

Washington Redskins' tailback Cliff Battles led the National Football League in rushing in 1937, his final season. He gained 137 more yards than in his previous best season.

6. STERLING SHARPE

Green Bay wide receiver Sterling Sharpe retired after the 1994 season with a career-ending spinal injury. Sharpe led the NFL in touchdown receptions that season with 18, catching 94 passes for 1,119 yards.

7. PETE PIHOS

Pete Pihos was one of the best ends of the 1950's. The Philadelphia Eagles' receiver led the NFL in receptions in 1955. In fact, he led the league in that category his final three seasons.

8. DON HUTSON

Green Bay end Don Hutson went out on top in 1945 by leading the NFL in receptions with 47. The amazing Hutson led the league in receptions eight times, including his final five seasons.

9. BUD GRANT

In 1952, Philadelphia Eagles' end Bud Grant caught 56 passes for 997 yards in his final NFL season. Those were the only catches the future Minnesota Vikings coach had in the league.

10. DAVEY O'BRIEN

Davey O'Brien, a quarterback for the Philadelphia Eagles, led the National Football League in pass completions in 1940. In his final game he set a record with 33 completions.

FANTASTIC FINISHES

Let's close the book by recalling some of the most exciting finishes in football history.

1. DOUG FLUTIE

Boston College trailed Miami 45–40 in the closing seconds on November 23, 1984. With the ball at the Miami 48-yard line, Boston College quarterback Doug Flutie had time for one more play. Flutie faded back and threw the ball more than 60 yards into the end zone. Receiver Gerald Phelan caught the desperation pass for a miracle touchdown as Boston College stunned Miami 47–45. For the game, Flutie completed 34 of 46 passes for 472 yards and three touchdowns. A week later Flutie was awarded the Heisman Trophy.

2. THE IMMACULATE RECEPTION

Twenty-two seconds remained in the 1972 American Conference Divisional Playoff game between the Oakland Raiders and the Pittsburgh Steelers. Trailing 7–6, Pittsburgh faced a fourth-and-ten situation on its own 40-yard line. Quarterback Terry Bradshaw threw a pass over the middle to running back Frenchy Fuqua. Just as the ball arrived, Raiders' defensive back Jack Tatum slammed into Fuqua. The ball popped into the air and it appeared that it would be an incomplete pass. In full stride, running back Franco Harris caught the ball right before it hit the ground at the Oakland 42-yard line and ran for the game-winning touchdown.

3. THE HAIL MARY PASS

It appeared that the Dallas Cowboys would need a miracle to win their 1975 National Conference Divisional Playoff game with the Minnesota Vikings. The Cowboys had the ball at midfield and were down 14–10. Only 32 seconds remained when quarterback Roger Staubach threw a pass toward the end zone. Receiver Drew Pearson outfought the Vikings' defenders and caught the ball to give Dallas an unbelievable last-second victory. Watching the game at home, the father of Viking quarterback Fran Tarkenton suffered a fatal heart attack. Staubach called the miraculous play the "Hail Mary" pass.

4. THE HOLY ROLLER

The San Diego Chargers led the Oakland Raiders 20–14 with ten seconds left on September 10, 1978. The Raiders had the ball at the Chargers' 14-yard line. Quarterback Ken Stabler fumbled when he was tackled by Chargers' defensive end Fred Dean. Running back Pete Banaszak batted the ball toward the goal line. Tight end Dave Casper kicked it into the end zone and fell on the ball for a touchdown as the Raiders prevailed 21–20. The press dubbed the play the "Holy Roller," but the San Diego fans had another name for it: the "Immaculate Deception." As a result of the play, the National Football League changed its rules so that a fumble couldn't be advanced in the final minutes of a game.

5. **TOM DEMPSEY**

Born with only half a right foot, Tom Dempsey of the New Orleans Saints seemed an unlikely choice to kick the longest field goal in NFL history. On November 8, 1970, Dempsey's Saints trailed the Detroit Lions 17–16 when the kicker was sent in to attempt a 63-yard field goal. The previous record for a field goal was 56 yards. Everyone was shocked when the ball sailed through the uprights to win the game.

6. **THE 1939 ROSE BOWL**

Duke entered their 1939 Rose Bowl game against the University of Southern California undefeated and unscored upon. It appeared that they might keep their perfect season intact as they led 3–0 in the fourth quarter. With just 41 seconds left on the clock, fourth-string USC quarterback Doyle Nave tossed a 19-yard touchdown pass to backup receiver Al Krueger to give the Trojans a 7–3 victory and ruin Duke's perfect season.

7. **HARVARD**

Both Harvard and Yale were undefeated when they met on October 23, 1968. Yale led 29–13 with only 42 seconds left to play. Reserve quarterback Frank Champi threw two touchdown passes in the final minute as Harvard escaped with a 29–29 tie. The Harvard newspaper headine read: HARVARD BEATS YALE 29–29.

8. **DWIGHT CLARK**

The Dallas Cowboys were beating the San Francisco Forty-Niners 27–21 in the 1981 National Conference Championship game when quarterback Joe Montana led the Forty-Niners on an 89-yard drive which culminated with wide receiver Dwight Clark's leaping fingertip catch with 51 seconds remaining. The reception gave San Francisco a thrilling 28–27 win and the play came to be known as "The Catch."

9. SUPER BOWL XXIII

The 1989 Super Bowl between the San Francisco Forty-Niners and the Cincinnati Bengals was one of the most exciting championship games ever. The Bengals led 16–13 late in the fourth quarter when the Forty-Niners began their final possession on their own eight-yard line. Masterfully, quarterback Joe Montana moved his team down the field. Wide receiver John Taylor caught a ten-yard touchdown pass with 34 seconds remaining to give San Francisco a 20–16 victory.

10. SUPER BOWL V

Super Bowl V was the first of many Super Bowl cliffhangers. The score was tied 13–13 with five seconds remaining when Baltimore place kicker Jim O'Brien lofted a 32-yard field goal to lift the Colts to a 16–13 victory over the Dallas Cowboys.

Bibliography

Barron, Bill. *The Official NFL Encyclopedia of Pro Football.* New York: New American Library, 1982.

Baxter, Russell and John Hassen. *ESPN The Ultimate Pro Football Guide.* New York: Hyperion, 1998.

Benedict, Jeff and Don Yaeger. *Pros and Cons.* New York: Warner, 1998.

Carroll, Bob and Michael Gershman. *Total Football II.* New York: HarperCollins, 1999.

Carruth, Gorton and Eugene Ehrlich. *Facts & Dates of American Sports.* New York: Perennial, 1988.

Clark, Patrick. *Sports Firsts.* New York: Facts on File, 1981.

Cohen, Richard and Jordan Duetsch. *The Scrapbook History of Pro Football.* Indianapolis: Bobbs Merrill, 1976.

Deitch, Scott. *The Official 1999 Football Records Book.* Indianapolis: NCAA, 1999.

Dobler, Conrad and Vic Carruci. *They Call Me Dirty.* New York: G.P. Putnam's Son, 1988.

Fischer, Stan and Shirley Fischer. *The Best, Worst, and Most Unusual in Sports.* New York: Fawcett Crest, 1977.

Gifford, Barry and Lawrence Lee. *Jack's Book.* New York: St. Martin's, 1978.

Gill, Bob, *Pro Football Trivia.* Chicago: Masters Press, 1999.

Hickok, Ralph. *A Who's Who of Sports Champions.* Boston: Houghton Mifflin, 1995.

Hofstede, David. *Slammin.* Toronto: ECW Press, 1999.

Hoppel, Joe. *The Sporting News Football Trivia Book.* St. Louis: Sporting News, 1985.

McNeil, Alex. *Total Television.* New York: Penguin, 1996.

Mendell, Ronald and Timothy Phares. *Who's Who in Football.* New Rochelle: Arlington House, 1974.

Nash, Bruce and Allan Zullo. *The Football Hall of Shame.* New York: Pocket Books, 1986.

——. *The Football Hall of Shame 2.* New York: Pocket Books, 1990.

Nixon, Richard. *The Memoirs of Richard Nixon.* New York: Grosset & Dunlap, 1978.

Porter, David. *Biographical Dictionary of American Sports: Football.* Westport: Greenwood Press, 1987.

Rathet, Mike and Don Smith. *Their Deeds and Dogged Faith.* New York: Rutledge Books, 1984.

Smith, Ron. *Football's 100 Greatest Players.* St. Louis: Sporting News, 1999.

Snyder, John. *Touchdown.* San Francisco: Chronicle, 1992.

Snyder, John and Floyd Conner. *Day By Day in Cincinnati Bengals History.* New York: Leisure, 1984.

Turnbull, Andrew. *Scott Fitzgerald.* New York: Ballantine, 1971.

Wallace, Irving and David Wallechinsky. *The Book of Lists 2.* New York: William Morrow, 1980.

Wallechinsky, David and Irving Wallace. *The People's Almanac 2.* New York: Bantam, 1978.

Ward, Gene and Dick Hyman. *Football Wit & Humor.* New York: Grosset & Dunlap, 1970.

Whittingham, Richard. *What a Game They Played.* New York: Harper & Row, 1984.

Yee, Min. *The Sports Book.* New York: Holt Rinehart and Winston, 1975.

Index

Abbott, Faye, 152
Abramowicz, Dan, 64
Afonse, Julie, 151
Age, Louis, 106
Agganis, Harry, 26
Aikman, Troy, 212
Alexander, Kermit, 126
Allen, George, 111, 159, 241
Allen, Marcus, 57
Alm, Jeff, 261
Alworth, Lance, 80
Alzado, Lyle, 10
Anderson, Ken, 188
Anderson, Willie, 122
Andrews, William, 54
Angsman, Elmer, 123
Arab Bowl, 2, 184
Arbanas, Fred, 217
Archer, Troy, 263
Asher, Bud, 75
Atkins, Doug, 113
Atkinson, Butch, 50
Auburn War Eagle, 94
Austin, Steve, 39
Awtrey, Alonzo, 239
Badgro, Morris, 26, 81
Baker, Terry, 32, 57
Ball, Larry, 129
Banaszak, Pete, 268
Barber, Mike, 90
Barrett, Ed, 216
Bass, Mike, 148
Battles, Cliff, 43, 76, 265
Baugh, Sammy, 10, 76, 130, 142
Bauman, Charlie, 237
Bausch, Jim, 34
Bayne, T.L., 2, 183
Beban, Gary, 58
Bednarik, Chuck, 131, 226
Beebe, Don, 197
Belichick, Steve, 121
Bell, Bert, 76, 243, 259
Bell, Ricky, 124
Bell, Tommy, 217
Bellino, Joe, 58
Berry, Charlie, 26
Berry, Raymond, 62
Berwanger, Jay, 6, 77
Bethel High School, 160
Bevo, 3, 95

Bezdek, Hugo, 127
Big Bear, 171
Biletnikoff, Fred, 80
Billups, Lewis, 250
Billy Goat, 95
Bingham, Gregg, 92
Bisaillon, Chris, 134
Blackwood, Lyle, 51, 91
Blanda, George, 2, 62, 141, 151
Bleier, Rocky, 216
Blinn College, 51
Blood, Johnny, 43, 85, 113, 118
Blozis, Al, 263
Bond, Ward, 17
Booth, Albie, 104
Borchert, Bill, 137
Bosley, Bruce, 146
Bosworth, Brian, 10, 88
Bowden, Timon, 239
Bows-O, 97
Boys Ranch Bowl, 169
Bradley, Bill, 234
Bradley, Luther, 122
Bradley, Phil, 25
Bradshaw, Terry, 197, 267
Brewer, Ed, 240
Brooks, James, 146
Brown, Bill, 229
Brown, Dante, 137
Brown, Eddie, 49
Brown, Hardy, 230
Brown, Jim, 12, 53, 64, 264
Brown, Johnny Mack, 13
Brown, Larry, 212
Brown, Larry, 217
Brown, Mike, 77, 196
Brown, Orlando, 107
Brown, Paul, 7, 75, 77, 99, 196
Brown, Reggie, 224
Brown, Ron, 35
Brown, Roosevelt, 62
Brown, Tom, 26
Brown, Willie, 66
Browner, Ross, 248
Brunell, Mark, 65
Bryan, Billy, 198
Bryant, Bear, 81
Bugel, Joe, 152
Bull, Scott, 151
Buncom, Frank, 258
Bunnell, Phil, 147
Burford, Chris, 253
Burkett, Jeff, 55
Butkus, Dick, 10, 15, 58, 88, 208, 232
Butts, Wally, 157
Byrd, Dennis, 223
Byrne, Eugene, 258

Cain, J.V., 259
Callahan, B.O., 179
Cal Poly–San Luis Obispo College, 260
Camp, Walter, 5, 233
Campbell, Earl, 57, 93, 209
Campbell, Marion, 154
Campbell, Milt, 36
Cannon, Billy, 252
Card-Pitt, 161
Carlson, George, 20
Carnegie Tech, 200
Carr, Henry, 34
Carruth, Rae, 250
Carter, Dayton, 166
Carter, Ki-Jana, 55
Carter, Michael, 36
Casey, Bernie, 13
Casper, Dave, 110, 268
Centre College, 25, 199
Champi, Frank, 269

Chandler, Don, 194
Chandler, Wes, 94
Chapman, Sam, 25
Chicken, Fred, 235
Chigger Bowl, 2, 170
Chipley, Bill, 196
Cigar Bowl, 191
Cincinnati Reds, 161
Cisco, Galen, 26
Clark, Al, 182
Clark, Algy, 152
Clark, Dutch, 33, 217
Clark, Dwight, 60, 269
Clark, Wayne, 150
Clements, Earle, 20
Cleveland, Grover, 184
College All Star Game, 188
Collier, Steve, 107
Collins, Kerry, 236
Columbia Marching Band, 176
Columbus Panhandles, 5, 173
Comp, Irv, 151
Conerly, Charlie, 195
Connor, George, 132
Constable, Pepper, 6
Conzelman, Jimmy, 42
Cook, Ed, 2, 179
Cook, Greg, 53
Copeland, John, 50
Corbus, Bill, 43
Cosby, Bill, 15, 16
Covert, Jim, 37
Crafts, Jerry, 106
Craig, Roger, 224
Croft, Tiny, 51
Crowley, Jim, 78
Csonka, Larry, 90, 146
Cumberland College, 164
Cunningham, W.A., 239
Cuozzo, Gary, 229
Currivan, Don, 138
Curtis, Mike, 228

Dale, Carroll, 232
Daniels, Jack, 104
Daniels, Jerome, 106
Dark, Alvin, 25
Darling, Boob, 51
Davidson, Cotton, 253
Davis, Ernie, 53
Davis, Glenn, 36
Davis, Glenn, 119, 133
Davis, Terrell, 202
Davis, Willie, 63
Dawkins, Pete, 42
Dayton Triangles, 5, 162
Deadeye, 171
Dean, Fred, 268
De Bartolo, Edward, 244
Decatur Staleys, 173, 235
Deer Slayer, Dick, 171
De Georgia, Jarrod, 134
Delaney, Joe, 55
Dempsey, Tom, 120, 216, 269
Devine, Dan, 221
Dick, Leo, 182
Dickerson, Eric, 209
Dick the Bruiser, 38
Dickey, James, 47
Dierdorf, Dan 91, 229
Dillon, Bobby, 217
Dillon, Corey, 55
Dilweg, Lavern, 20
Ditka, Mike, 79, 85
Dixon, David, 105, 106
Dobie, Gil, 155
Dobler, Conrad, 91, 234
Docherty, Jim, 180
Doehring, Bull, 181
Donelli, Aldo, 127

Donovan, Art, 109, 115
Dorais, Gus, 103
Dorsett, Tony, 57
Douglass, Bobby, 140
Dowd, Snooks, 180
Dowler, Boyd, 210, 232
Downs, Gary, 83
Downwind, Xavier, 171
Dressen, Chuck, 25
Driscoll, Paddy, 26
Dryer, Fred, 17
Dudley, Bill, 131
Dugat, Gentry, 164
Duhe, A.J., 122
Duluth Eskimos, 98, 172
Duncan, Randy, 57

Eagle Feather, 171
Edwards, Herman, 146
Edwards, Turk, 2, 219
Eisenhower, Dwight, 2, 21
Elway, John, 75, 198
Esiason, Boomer, 78
Essegian, Chuck, 25
Estabrook, Jay, 147
Eubank, Weeb, 128
Evans, Dippy, 122
Evans, Norm, 100

Fallon, Gary, 220
Farrington, Bo, 263
Favre, Brett, 10, 65
Fears, Tom, 64, 139
Feathers, Beattie, 124, 141
Feldman, Marty, 152
Ferguson, Joe, 140
Fernandez, Manny, 90
Ferrum College, 50
Filchock, Frank, 243
Fischer, Pat, 60
Fish Bowl, 2, 169
Fish, Hamilton, 24
Fitzgerald, Scott, 46
Flaherty, Ray, 100, 255
Flutie, Doug, 267
Fog Bowl, 189
Follis, Charles, 69
Ford, Gerald, 2, 21, 101, 111
Fortmann, Dan, 41
Foster, Barry, 125
Fralic, Bill, 37
Francis, Joe, 61
Francis, Russ, 37
Frankford Yellow Jackets, 174
Frerotte, Gus, 59, 220
Friesell, Red, 191
Fuqua, Frenchy, 231, 267

Gabriel, Roman, 111
Gaines, Clark, 83
Galimore, Willie, 263
Gallaudet College, 217
Gardiner, William, 20
Garman, Harry, 180
Garvey, Steve, 26
Gastineau, Mark, 37, 119
Gatewood, Randy, 137
Gatlin, Larry, 165
Gayle, Shaun, 198
Gehrke, Fred, 101
Gent, Pete, 46
George, Phyllis, 92, 215
Georgia Tech University, 164, 253
Gibbs, Jake, 25
Gibron, Abe, 154
Gibson, Bob, 146
Giel, Paul, 25
Gifford, Frank, 10, 18, 117, 226, 235
Ging, Jack, 19
Gipp, George, 23, 261
Gipson, Paul, 165

Glanville, Jerry, 176, 177
Glassic, Tom, 198
Glenn, Howard, 258
Gogolak, Charlie, 180, 185
Gogolak, Pete, 8
Goldberg, Bill, 38
Gowdy, Curt, 214
Graham, Otto, 29, 128, 140, 185, 231
Grange, Red, 20, 80, 103, 115, 130, 156, 235
Grant, Bud, 31, 203, 266
Graves, Bibb, 20
Gray Horse, 171
Green, Roy, 130
Green, Tim, 45
Green, Trent, 65
Greene, Joe, 234, 235
Greene, Kevin, 37
Grier, Rosey, 10, 63
Griese, Bob, 148
Griffin, Archie, 128
Grimm, Russ, 87
Gross, Sammy, 241
Gumbo, 96
Gustavus Adolphus College, 51

Haggerty, Pat, 194
Halas, George, 28, 113, 130, 154, 156, 174, 222, 231, 236
Halloran, Bill, 194
Handler, Phil, 153
Hapes, Merle, 243
Harbaugh, Jim, 215
Harmon, Mark, 18
Harmon, Tom, 51, 56
Harris, Franco, 231, 268
Hart, Jim, 182
Hart, Leon, 220
Harvard University, 24, 25, 98, 147, 159, 176, 199, 233, 239, 258, 269
Haugsrud, Ole, 172
Havlicek, John, 29
Hayes, Bob, 35
Hayes, Lester, 22
Hayes, Woody, 236
Heffelfinger, Pudge, 6
Heidi Game, 213
Hein, Mel, 132
Heisman, John, 114, 164, 253
Henderson, Hollywood, 88, 92, 110, 248
Henderson, Keith, 252
Henderson, Mark, 240
Hendricks, Ted, 87, 114
Henley, Darryl, 250
Henry, Mike, 14
Herron, Mack, 104
Herschberger, Clarence, 108
Hersey, John, 47
Hill, Mack Lee, 258
Hinds Community College, 50
Hines, Jim, 34
Hinkle, Clarke, 232
Hinkley, Frank, 233
Hirsch, Elroy, 78, 226
Hoerner, Dick, 230
Hoernschemeyer, Hunchy, 178
Hogan, Jim, 147
Holden, Sam, 83
Holmes, Ernie, 37
Holy Cross University, 201
Hornibrook, John, 181
Hornung, Paul, 57, 118, 243
Houston, Jim, 229
Howard, Desmond, 211
Howard, Perry, 121
Howard, Tubby, 51
Howley, Chuck, 212
Hoying, Bobby, 150
Huarte, John, 58
Hubbard, Cal, 26
Hucul, Bud, 74

Hughes, Chuck, 257
Hultz, Don, 139
Hurt, Eric, 82
Hutson, Don, 132, 265

Ice Bowl, 187, 188
Iodine Bowl, 2, 168
Irsay, Robert, 75
Isbell, Cecil, 218, 265
Izo, George, 121

Jackson, Bo, 26, 59
Jackson, Frank, 232
Jackson, Johnny, 121
Jackson, Keith, 214
Jackson, Ransom, 26
Jacobs, Jack, 56
Jacoby, Joe, 67
Janowicz, Vic, 28
Jenkins, Alfred, 50
Jennings, Stanford, 212
Jensen, Jackie, 26
Johnson, Anthony, 125
Johnson, Harvey, 153
Johnson, Lyndon, 101
Johnson, Pete, 248
Johnson, Stone, 258
Johnson, Walter, 37
Johnsos, Luke, 181
Jones, Biter, 235
Jones, Calvin, 56
Jones, Deacon, 63, 209
Jones, Jerry, 252
Jones, Johnny Lam, 36
Jones, K.C., 32
Jones, Larry, 157
Joss, Johnny, 147
Jurgensen, Sonny, 264
Kapp, Joe, 229
Karras, Alex, 18, 37, 45, 81, 89, 234, 243
Kazmaier, Dick, 42
Keeling, Rex, 196
Kelly, Jim, 128, 215
Kelly, Leroy, 64
Kelly, Shipwreck, 116, 244
Kemp, Jack, 2, 21
Kennedy, John, 42, 48
Kennedy, Ted, 2, 22
Kenney, Bill, 52
Kerouac, Jack, 46
Keyes, Leroy, 132
Khayat, Bob, 182
Kickapoo Bowl, 2, 169
Kiesling, Walt, 61, 153
Kiick, Jim, 82
Kilmer, Billy, 111, 146
King, J.V., 241
King, Kenny, 211
King, Larry, 214
Kinnick, Nile, 56
Kirksey, Jon, 106
Klecko, Joe, 10
Klingler, David, 134, 135
Kluszewski, Ted, 26
Kramer, Jerry, 218
Krause, Paul, 192
Kristofferson, Kris, 10
Krueger, Al, 269
Krueger, Charlie, 91
Krumrie, Tim, 224
Kuharich, Joe, 114
Kunz, George, 43
Kush, Frank, 158

Ladd, Ernie, 40
Lambeau, Curley, 114
Lamonica, Daryle, 80
Landeta, Sean, 198
Lane, Dick, 66, 142, 232
Langer, Jim, 67
Largent, Steve, 2, 22

Lary, Yale, 20
Lasher, Tim, 97
Lassa, Nikolas, 73
Lattner, Johnny, 197
Laughing Gas, 171
Layden, Elmer, 78, 98
Layne, Bobby, 227
Leahy, Frank, 197, 239
Leslie, Harry, 20
Lett, Leon, 50, 197
Levy, Marv, 203
Lewis, Tommy, 238
Lewis, William Henry, 69
Lilly, Bob, 148
Lingo, Walter, 73
Lipscomb, Gene, 37, 246
Little Twig, Joe, 171
Livingston, Bob, 220
Livingston, Dale, 196
Lom, Benny, 145
Lomax, Neil, 165
Lombardi, Vince, 61, 64, 112, 152, 154
Lone Wolf, Ted, 171
Long, Chuck, 59
Long, Howie, 10
Longley, Clint, 120
Long Time Sleep, 171
Looney, Joe Don, 86
Losch, Jack, 61
Lothridge, Billy, 218
Lott, Ronnie, 233
Luger, Lex, 37
Lundy, Lamar, 63
Lusteg, Booth, 255
Lynch, Dick, 201

Macalester College, 162
Mack, Connie, 185
Macleish, Archibald, 47
Majkowski, Don, 125
Majors, Lee, 18
Manaco, Fran, 75
Manley, Dexter, 247
Mansfield, Ray, 233
Mara, Tim, 244
Marchetti, Gino, 114
Marinaro, Ed, 17
Marino, Dan, 138, 143, 144, 206, 207
Marshall, George Preston, 76, 118, 166
Marshall, Jim, 145, 229
Marshall, Rube, 70
Marshall University, 165, 260
Martin, Harvey, 37
Martin, Rod, 211
Mason, Frank, 113
Mathewson, Christy, 185
Mathias, Bob, 36
Matson, Ollie, 35
Matte, Tom, 221
Matuszak, John, 10, 114
Mauldin, Stan, 258
McAllester, Sam, 240
McBride, Art, 77
McCaffrey, Ed, 236
McCarthy, John, 149
McDaniel, Wahoo, 40
McElhenny, Hugh, 216, 231
McGee, Max, 210
McHan, Lamar, 61
McKay, Bob, 235
McKay, John, 161
McMahon, Jim, 89
McMichael, Steve, 37, 40
McMillan, Bo, 199
McQueen, Butch, 164
McWhorter, Bob, 189
Meeker, Butch, 102
Meehan, Chuck, 240
Mehringer, Pete, 34

Metzger, Charles, 166
Meyer, Monk, 6
Michalik, Art, 150
Miller, Don, 78
Mitchell, Bobby, 76, 121
Mix, Ron, 44
Modell, Art, 75
Moegle, Dicky, 238
Moen, Kevin, 180
Monot, Dodo, 258
Montana, Joe, 93, 147, 151, 207, 269, 270
Moore, Bobby, 182
Moran, Charlie, 25
Morrall, Earl, 205
Morris, Bam, 247
Morris Brown College, 50
Morris, Glenn, 34
Morris, Mercury, 108, 246
Morris, Tom, 142
Morton, Craig, 204
Moss, Randy, 251, 252
Motley, Marion, 72
Mudd, Howard, 91
Muncie, Chuck, 247
Munns, Dave, 155
Munoz, Anthony, 208
Murphy, Bill, 191
Mutryn, Chet, 192

Nagurski, Bronko, 38, 232
Namath, Joe, 14, 58, 116, 200, 245
Naumetz, Frank, 100
Navarro Junior College, 49
Nave, Doyle, 269
Neale, Greasy, 28
Nelsen, Bill, 227
Nelson, Al, 139
Nelson, Ozzie, 15
Nesser, Al, 175
Nesser, Charles, 173
Nesser, Frank, 173
Nesser, Fred, 173
Nesser, John, 173
Nesser, Phil, 173
Nesser, Ted, 173
Nevers, Ernie, 27, 228
Newman, Wallace, 23
New Mexico Military Institute, 51
Nixon, Mike, 153
Nixon, Richard, 21, 23, 159
Nomellini, Leo, 37, 131
Norton, Jerry, 140
Norwood, Scott, 205
Nottingham, Don, 78

Oberlander, Swede, 178
O'Brien, Davey, 102
O'Brien, Jim, 212, 266, 270
O'Connell, Tommy, 139
Olsen, Merlin, 17, 63, 234
O'Neal, Steve, 138
Oorang Indians, 1, 73, 74, 112, 171
Orr, Jimmy, 205
Otto, Jim, 227
Owen, Steve, 100, 232
Owens, R.C., 182
Owens, Steve, 125

Pacific Glass Works, 257
Paige, Stephone, 52
Parker, Ace, 25, 228
Paschal, Bill, 67
Patten, Haden, 241
Payton, Walter, 79, 93, 138
Peabody, Endicott, 24
Pearson, Drew, 193, 268
Pearson, Preston, 60
Perry, William, 37, 79, 105
Peters, Forrest, 136

Peterson, Bill, 153
Phelan, Gerald, 267
Phillips, Leon, 20
Piccolo, Brian, 261
Pietrzak, Jim, 234
Pihos, Pete, 265
Pillman, Brian, 37
Pinchot, Gifford, 20
Pingel, Scott, 137
Pisarcik, Joe, 146
Pleasant, R.G., 20
Plimpton, George, 45
Plunkett, Jim, 57, 181, 211
Poe, Arthur, 47
Poe, Edgar Allan, 47, 99
Poe, John, 47
Poe, Neilson, 47
Poe, Samuel, 47
Poinsettia Bowl, 168
Pollard, Fritz, 70
Poole, Barney, 195
Poole, Ray, 197
Pope, Bucky, 125
Pope, Lew, 149
Pottsville Maroons, 172
Price, Mike, 88
Pritchard, Ron, 37
Providence Steam Roller, 8, 42, 173
Pugh, Jethro, 148
Pyle, G.E., 192

Quick, Mike, 82
Quinby, Bill, 193

Racine Cardinals, 1, 172
Racine Legion, 1, 174
Rashad, Ahmad, 214
Ratterman, George, 99
Ray, John, 105
Reader, Russ, 45
Reagan, Ronald, 23
Reaves, John, 181
Rechichar, Bert, 120
Reck, Dennis, 160
Red Fang, 171
Reed, Andre, 128
Reeves, Dan, 204
Refrigerator Bowl, 2, 169
Reich, Frank, 128
Remington, Frederic, 229
Reveille, 96
Reynolds, Billy, 230
Reynolds, Burt, 12
Reynolds, Jack, 79
Rice, Jerry, 22, 132, 136, 147, 166
Richter, Les, 129, 236
Riegels, Roy, 145
Riley, Pat, 29
Ringo, Jim, 154
Ripon College, 50
Roach, Rollin, 104
Roberson, Bo, 35
Robinson, Jackie, 27, 69, 70, 71
Robustelli, Andy, 63
Rochester Jeffersons, 163, 174
Rock, The, 38
Rockne, Knute, 23, 200, 261
Rogers, Don, 246
Rogers, Reggie, 250
Romanowski, Bill, 236
Rooney, Art, 244
Roosevelt, Theodore, 257
Rosenbloom, Carroll, 75
Rossi, Cal, 76
Rossovich, Tim, 10, 85, 92
Running Deer, David, 171
Rush, Clive, 2, 219
Rush, Tyrone, 82
Rushing, Marion, 82
Rust, Rod, 152

Rutgers University, 7, 15, 42
Rutledge, Kevin, 158

Sachs, Allan, 111
Sack, Jack, 83
Saddleback Junior College, 52
Salad Bowl, 170
Sample, Johnny, 235
Sanders, Barry, 57, 207
Sanders, Carl, 20
Sanders, Deion, 27, 130
Sandifer, Don, 126
Sayers, Gale, 54, 208, 226, 261
Scanlon, Dewey, 172
Schachter, Norm, 193
Schlichter, Art, 242
Schlick, Leo, 134
Schmidt, Francis, 3, 220
Schnellbacher, Otto, 31
Schottenheimer, Marty, 236
Scott, Clair, 182
Scott, Jake, 111
Seal, 96
Sebastian the Ibis, 94
Seibold, Champ, 51
Sestak, Tom, 60
Settle, John, 68
Shakespeare, Bill, 6
Sharpe, Sterling, 224, 225, 265
Shaw, Dennis, 136
Shaw, George, 61
Shay, Brian, 136
Shell, Art, 71
Shula, Dave, 77, 154
Shula, Don, 77, 90, 109, 154, 159, 239
Shuler, Heath, 59
Simmons, Ron, 39
Simpson, O.J., 13, 57, 58, 117, 132, 208, 209, 233, 249
Sims, David, 126
Sipe, Brian, 136
Sistrunk, Otis, 89
Sligh, Richard, 129
Smith, Bubba, 10, 15
Smith, Emmett, 212
Smith, Jackie, 92, 204
Smith, John, 240
Smith, Noland, 103
Smith, Timmy, 210
Smith, Tommie, 34, 221
Snavely, Carl, 191
Snow Bowl, 187
Soar, Hank, 32
Sonnenberg, Gus, 39, 105
Sooner Schooner, 96
Spaghetti Bowl, 2, 170
Speedie, Mac, 84
Spikes, Jack, 83
Sprinkle, Ed, 231
Squirek, Jack, 211
Stabler, Ken, 148, 268
Stagg, Amos Alonzo, 108
Staley, A.E., 173
Stanford Marching Band, 176
Starr, Bart, 61, 187
Staubach, Roger, 51, 57, 120, 121, 193, 204, 215, 264, 268
St. Clair, Bob, 111
Stearns, John, 26
Sternaman, Joey, 103
Stingley, Darryl, 223, 231
Stirnweiss, Snuffy, 26
Stone, Harlan, 41
Story, Bill, 45
Stringer, Korey, 106
Strode, Woody, 10, 71
Strong, Ken, 255
Stuhldreher, Harry, 43, 78
Sullivan, Arthur, 179

Sullivan, Pat, 58
Swann, Eric, 9
Switzer, Barry, 252

Taliaferro, Gorge, 71
Talmadge, Eugene, 20
Tarkenton, Fran, 205, 208, 268
Tattersoll, Jack, 70
Tatum, Jack, 223, 231, 268
Taylor, Blondie, 166
Taylor, John, 270
Taylor, Lawrence, 37, 224, 248
Taylor, Lionel, 222
Teaff, Grant, 109
Terry, Wyllys, 175
Terzian, Armen, 193
Theismann, Joe 41, 224
Thomas, Derrick, 261, 262
Thomas, Duane, 247
Thomas, Thurman, 205
Thomas, Tra, 106
Thomason, Stumpy, 145
Thompson, Jack, 126
Thor, 95
Thorpe, Jim, 21, 26, 35, 73, 245
Thrower, Willie, 71, 83
Thunder, Baptiste, 171
Timberlake, Bob, 150
Tillman, Rusty, 111
Tinker, Gerald, 34
Tittle, Y.A., 182, 195, 230
Tobin, Elgie, 70
Tomahawk Arrowhead, 171
Tomey, Dick, 156
Tonawanda Kardex, 174
Toretta, Gino, 59
Tose, Leonard, 244
Totten, William, 136, 166
Trafton, George, 235
Triplett, Wally, 8
Tunnell, Emlen, 66
Turkey Bowl, 2, 169
Turner, Bulldog, 131
Twilley, Howard, 232
Tyrer, Jim, 249

Unitas, Johnny, 2, 60, 144, 221, 228
University of the South, 2, 175, 220
Utley, Mike, 223

Van Buren, Steve, 25
Vannemann, Reeve, 180
Van Oelhoffen, Kimo, 51
Varrichone, Frank, 239
Vaught, John, 158

Waddell, Rube, 185
Walla Walla Community College, 51
Walls, Everson, 67
Ward, Charlie, 29, 30
War Eagle, 171
Ware, Andre, 59
Warfield, Paul, 159
Warmuth, Murray, 255
Warner, Pop, 99, 238
Warner, Kurt, 1, 65, 144
Warren, Chris, 50
Washington, Kenny, 10, 70
Waterfield, Bob, 119
Watts, J.C., 2, 22
Wayne, John, 11, 12
Weathers, Carl, 13
Wedemeyer, Herman, 19
Wells, Warren, 80
Wersching, Ray, 147
Wham, Tom, 84
Wheeler, Cowboy, 51
Whelan, Tommy, 192

White Cloud, 171
White, Reggie, 37
White, Whizzer, 41
Widby, Ron, 32
Williams. Travis, 142
Williamson, Fred, 14, 232
Wilson, Larry, 227
Wilson, Mike, 129
Wilson, Red, 26, 179
Wilson, Tim, 93
Wismer, Harry, 74
Wistert, Alvin, 176
Witmer, Dave, 180
Wolmas, Woodchuck, 171
Wood, Willie, 67
Woodley, David, 206
Woodruff, George, 158, 189
Woods, Ickey, 55
Woods, Jerome, 236
Wright, Lonnie, 31
Wyche, Sam, 146

Yale University, 21, 47, 147, 229, 233, 269
Yandell, Bobby, 197
Yepremian, Garo, 148
Yost, Fielding, 157
Young, Buddy, 102
Younger, Tank, 236

Zabel, Baldy, 192
Zatkoff, Zany, 231
Zuppke, Robert, 156, 200

About the Author

Floyd Conner is a lifelong football fan and the author of eleven books. His sports books include *Baseball's Most Wanted, Day By Day in Cincinnati Bengals History,* and *This Date in Sports History.* He also co-authored *Day By Day in Cincinnati Reds History* and the best-selling *365 Sports Facts a Year Calendar.* He lives in Cincinnati with his wife, Susan, and son, Travis.